Cybersecurity Fundamentals Explained

Brian Mackay

Published by Brian Mackay, 2024.

Table of Contents

C

INTRODUCTION

The issue of Cybersecurity is of paramount importance in the digital age. With near continuous revelations about incidents and breaches in the media, organizations and individuals are faced with the challenge of finding the balance between risk, innovation, and cost. At the same time, the field of cyber security is undergoing dramatic changes, demanding that organizations embrace new practices and skill sets.

In this book, I will explore the basics of Cybersecurity and discuss how ordinary people and organizations can best ensure the safety and security of their data. By examining numerous studies, reports, and surveys, I will argue that organizations must embrace a comprehensive approach to cyber security that considers the ever-changing nature of the threat landscape.

In the following chapters, I will first explain the fundamentals of cyber security, then discuss several case studies on the more prominent security breaches in the last few years to show what can happen to a business.

PART 1 – THE FUNDAMENTALS OF CYBERSECURITY

Cybersecurity fundamentals refer to the core principles and practices that are essential for protecting computer systems, networks, and data from unauthorized access, cyber threats, and data breaches. These fundamentals form the basis of a strong cybersecurity posture and are crucial for individuals and organizations alike. Here are some key cybersecurity fundamentals:

Confidentiality: Confidentiality ensures that sensitive information remains private and accessible only to authorized individuals. It involves implementing measures such as encryption, access controls, and secure communication channels to prevent unauthorized disclosure.

Integrity: Integrity ensures the accuracy, consistency, and trustworthiness of data and systems. It involves implementing mechanisms to prevent unauthorized modification, tampering, or corruption of data and ensuring that data remains intact and unaltered.

Availability: Availability ensures that systems, networks, and data are accessible and operational when needed. It involves implementing measures to prevent service disruptions, such as implementing backup and disaster recovery solutions, redundancy, and proactive monitoring to detect and address potential issues.

Authentication: Authentication verifies the identity of users, systems, or devices attempting to access a network or system. It involves the use of strong passwords, multi-factor authentication (MFA), biometrics, and other techniques to ensure that only authorized individuals or systems gain access.

Authorization: Authorization determines what actions or resources an authenticated user or system can access. It involves assigning appropriate permissions and privileges based on user roles and responsibilities to prevent unauthorized access or misuse of resources.

Risk Management: Risk management involves identifying, assessing, and mitigating potential cybersecurity risks. It includes conducting regular risk assessments, implementing security controls and safeguards, and developing incident response plans to minimize the impact of security incidents.

Security Awareness: Security awareness is about educating and training individuals to recognize and respond to potential cyber threats. It includes promoting good security practices, such as strong password hygiene, avoiding phishing emails and suspicious links, and being vigilant against social engineering tactics.

Vulnerability Management: Vulnerability management involves identifying and remediating security vulnerabilities in systems and software. It includes regularly patching and updating software, conducting vulnerability assessments and penetration testing, and promptly addressing identified weaknesses.

Security Monitoring: Security monitoring involves continuously monitoring systems, networks, and data for potential security breaches or anomalies. It includes implementing intrusion detection and prevention systems, log monitoring, and security information and event management (SIEM) solutions to detect and respond to security incidents in a timely manner.

Incident Response: Incident response is a planned approach to addressing and managing security incidents. It involves establishing an incident response team, developing incident response plans and playbooks, and conducting regular drills and exercises to ensure an effective response in the event of a security breach.

CYBERSECURITY FUNDAMENTALS EXPLAINED

These fundamentals provide a solid foundation for implementing a comprehensive cybersecurity strategy. However, it is important to note that cybersecurity is a rapidly evolving field, and staying updated with the latest threats, technologies, and best practices is crucial for maintaining a strong security posture.

Here are some basics of cybersecurity that you should know:

1. Passwords: Using secure passwords is important to protect your personal and sensitive information from unauthorized access. Here are some tips for creating and using secure passwords:

    1. **- Use a strong password: A strong password should be at least twelve characters long and include a combination of uppercase and lowercase letters, numbers, and Special characters.**
    2. **- Avoid using personal information: Don't use your name, birthdate, or other personal information in your password, as it can be easy for someone to guess.**
    3. **- Use different passwords for different accounts: Don't use the same password for multiple accounts. If one password is compromised, it can put all of your accounts at risk.**
    4. **- Don't share your password: Never share your password with anyone, including friends and family.**
    5. **- Use two-factor authentication: Many websites and services offer two-factor authentication (2FA), which requires you to enter a code generated by an authenticator app such as Google authenticator or a code sent to your smartphone or email in addition to your password giving you an extra layer of security.**
    6. **- Use a password manager: A password manager such as Nordpass can help you create and remember strong passwords for all of your online accounts saving them in a very secure vault.**

1.7 – Use of random words in a password – this can make it more secure against hacking attempts. Here are some tips on using random words effectively:

Use a long passphrase rather than a short password. For example, "correct horse battery staple" is more secure than "Tr0ub4dor&3".

Choose words randomly rather than a known phrase. Avoid common phrases, quotes, or song lyrics.

Use a mix of random words, numbers, and special characters. For example: "color179paperclip<>bicyclepotato"

Use a password generator tool to randomly combine words if needed. Diceware is a popular method that uses dice rolls to pick words from a list.

Use a combination of lowercase, uppercase, numbers and symbols. This increases the complexity against brute force attacks.

Avoid personal information, names, birthdays, or dictionary words. Make the words as random as possible.

Use a different random passphrase for each account. Don't reuse the same passphrase across multiple sites.

Consider using a password manager to store long, complex passphrases securely. This helps you avoid reusing or forgetting them.

Update passwords periodically, such as every 90 days. Changing a few words in your existing passphrase can help.

The key is using long, random strings of words and characters that only you know. This makes it extremely difficult for hackers to guess via brute force attacks.

• • • •

1. Anti-virus software:

ANTI-VIRUS SOFTWARE such as Avast, MacAfee, or Norton, is a type of computer program designed to detect, prevent, and remove malicious software, also known as malware, from a computer system. Malware can include viruses, trojan horses, worms, spyware, and adware, which can compromise the security of a computer system, steal data, or damage the system's files.

CYBERSECURITY FUNDAMENTALS EXPLAINED

Anti-virus software works by scanning the files and programs on a computer system, looking for known patterns or signatures of malware. When it finds a match, it either quarantines or deletes the infected file or program. Antivirus software also uses heuristics and behaviour-based detection to identify new and unknown threats that do not match any known malware signatures.

In addition to real-time scanning, many anti-virus software programs provide additional features such as firewalls, email filtering, and web protection. These features help to protect the computer system from several types of attacks and can prevent users from accidentally downloading or installing malicious software.

It is important to keep anti-virus software up to date with the latest virus definitions and software patches to ensure the best possible protection against new and emerging threats.

1. Firewalls:

A firewall is a network security device that monitors and controls incoming and outgoing network traffic based on predetermined security rules. Firewalls are used to protect a network from unauthorized access, and to prevent malware and other security threats from spreading through the network.

There are several types of firewalls, including:

3.1 Packet-filtering firewalls: These firewalls examine each packet of data that travels through the network and compare it to a set of predefined rules. If a packet matches the rules, it is allowed through the firewall. If not, it is blocked.

3.2 Stateful firewalls: These firewalls not only examine individual packets, but also keep track of the state of network connections. This enables them to allow incoming traffic that is part of an established connection, while blocking traffic that is not.

3.3 Application-level gateways: These firewalls inspect data at the application layer of the network protocol stack. They can block or allow specific types of traffic based on the application being used.

Firewalls are a vital component of network security and are commonly used in both home and enterprise networks. By controlling access to a network and monitoring network traffic, firewalls can help prevent unauthorized access and protect sensitive data from being compromised. However, firewalls are just one part of a comprehensive security strategy and should be used in conjunction with other security measures such as anti-virus software, intrusion detection systems, and regular security audits.

4. Software updates: Essential for ensuring the security, functionality, and performance of any software application. Here are some of the reasons why software updates are important:

4.1 Security: Software updates often include security patches that address vulnerabilities or bugs that could be exploited by cybercriminals. By keeping your software up to date, you reduce the risk of security breaches, data loss, and other cyber threats.

4.2 Improved functionality: Software updates often include new features, improvements, and bug fixes that can enhance the overall functionality of the software. This means you can enjoy a better user experience and increased productivity.

4.3 Performance: Updates can also improve the performance of the software by optimizing its code, improving its efficiency, and reducing memory usage. This can result in faster load times, better responsiveness, and smoother performance.

4.4 Compatibility: As technology evolves, software applications may become incompatible with newer hardware or operating systems. Software updates can ensure compatibility with the latest hardware and operating systems, which helps to extend the life of your software investment.

4.5 Support: Software vendors typically provide support only for the latest versions of their software. By staying up to date with software updates, you ensure that you are eligible for support when you need it.

Overall, software updates are crucial for maintaining the security, functionality, and performance of any software application. It is important to keep your software up to date to avoid potential issues and ensure that you are getting the most out of your software investment.

5. Backups - Essential for ensuring the safety and security of important data and information. They provide a way to recover data

in case of system failure, data corruption, cyber-attacks, or other unforeseen circumstances.

Here are some reasons why backups are important:

5.1 Protecting against data loss: Backups ensure that data is safe and can be restored in case of any data loss due to hardware or software failure, accidental deletion, or human error.

5.2 Mitigating the impact of cyber-attacks: Cyber-attacks like ransomware and malware can cause considerable damage to computer systems and data. Backups provide a way to recover from these attacks and minimize their impact.

5.3 Compliance with regulatory requirements: Many industries have strict regulatory requirements for data backup and retention. Backups can help organizations comply with these requirements and avoid penalties for non-compliance.

5.4 Facilitating disaster recovery: Backups are an essential part of disaster recovery planning. They provide a way to recover critical data and applications in case of a natural disaster or other catastrophic event.

5.5 Peace of mind: Knowing that data is safely backed up and can be recovered in case of any issues can provide peace of mind to individuals and organizations.

In summary, backups are crucial for data protection, business continuity, and compliance with regulations. They should be a part of any organization's data management strategy.

6. Phishing:

Phishing is a type of cyber-attack in which an attacker sends a fraudulent email, text message, or website that appears to be from a legitimate source in order to obtain sensitive information, such as usernames, passwords, credit card numbers, or other personal information. The goal of a phishing attack is to trick the victim into providing their information, which can then be used to commit identity theft, financial fraud, or other malicious activities.

Phishing attacks can be very convincing, often using social engineering techniques to create a sense of urgency or fear in the victim. For example, a phishing email might claim that the victim's account has been compromised and prompt them to click on a link to reset their password, which would then take them to a fake website that looks like the legitimate one. Alternatively, a phishing email might ask the victim to provide personal information for a legitimate reason, such as updating their account information or confirming a payment.

To protect yourself from phishing attacks, it is important to be cautious when opening emails or clicking on links from unknown or suspicious sources. Always verify the legitimacy of a website before entering any sensitive information, and never provide personal information in response to an unsolicited email or phone call. Additionally, using two-factor authentication and regularly updating your passwords can help to prevent unauthorized access to your accounts.

7. Social engineering:

Social engineering is a technique used to manipulate or influence people into taking actions that may not be in their best interest, often for malicious purposes. It involves exploiting people's trust, emotions, and natural tendencies to make them divulge sensitive information, perform certain actions, or grant access to restricted areas.

Social engineering can take many forms, including phishing attacks, pretexting, baiting, and tailgating. In a phishing attack, the attacker sends a fraudulent email or message that is from a trusted source, such as a bank or social media platform, and asks the recipient to provide sensitive information like passwords or credit card numbers. Pretexting involves creating a false identity or scenario to gain the trust of the target and extract sensitive information or access. Baiting involves leaving a tempting item, like a USB drive, in a public place, hoping that someone will pick it up and use it on their computer, thereby granting the attacker access to that computer. Tailgating involves following someone into a restricted area without proper authorization.

Social engineering attacks can be highly effective because they exploit people's natural tendencies, such as trust and helpfulness. It is important to be vigilant and cautious when interacting with others, especially when it comes to providing sensitive information or granting access to restricted areas. Awareness and education about social engineering can also help individuals and organizations protect themselves from these types of attacks.

8. Remote working / Remote access:

If you work remotely, use a secure virtual private network (VPN) to protect your online activity and data from unauthorized access by encrypting all date being transferred from your computer to the internet, your work's internal network and back.

Remote access is defined as the ability to connect and control a computer or network from a different location over the internet or a private network. It allows users to access files, applications, and other resources on a remote computer or network as if they were physically present in the same location.

Remote access can be achieved using various tools and technologies, including Remote Desktop Protocol (RDP), Virtual Private Network (VPN), and cloud-based services. It is commonly used by businesses to provide remote employees with access to company resources, such as files, databases, and applications, as well as to support remote collaboration and communication. However, remote access also poses security risks, as it can potentially allow unauthorized access to sensitive data and systems. To minimize these risks, it is important to use secure remote access methods, implement proper access controls, and regularly monitor and audit remote access activities.

• • • •

9. Cybersecurity awareness:

FINALLY, STAY INFORMED about the latest cybersecurity threats and best practices through online resources, training, and workshops. Stay vigilant and report any suspicious activity to your IT department or cybersecurity experts.

Cybersecurity awareness is defined as the knowledge, understanding, and practices that individuals and organizations use to protect themselves from online threats and attacks. It involves being aware of the several types of cyber threats, such as malware, phishing, ransomware, and social engineering, and taking proactive steps to prevent them.

Cybersecurity awareness involves staying informed about the latest security risks and vulnerabilities, understanding how to protect personal and sensitive information, and knowing how to respond to security incidents when they occur. It also involves using strong passwords, keeping software up-to-date, and being vigilant about suspicious emails, links, and messages.

Overall, cybersecurity awareness is an essential aspect of staying safe online, and it is critical for individuals and organizations to prioritize cybersecurity education and training to prevent cyber-attacks and protect sensitive data.

It is the practice of protecting sensitive data and critical systems from digital attacks is known as Cyber security. It is a clear strategy used to combat threats that affect an organization's business critical networked applications and systems.

According to IBM, the cost of a data breach in 2022 was around 3 million US Dollars in the US and over 5 USD million in the global market. These expenses include the cost of responding to the incident, the cost of downtime, and the long-term damage to a company's reputation.

In most cases, criminals obtain the personal information of customers, such as their names, addresses, email addresses, credit card numbers, and social security numbers. They then sell these records on the "dark web" such as underground digital platforms such as Tor. Compromised PII (Personally

Identifiable Information), can lead to various issues, such as the loss of customer trust and the imposition of legal actions.

The phrase "cyber security" refers to a range of situations, including commercial and mobile computers, and can be broken down into a few basic categories.

Network security - The act of protecting a computer network from intruders, including malicious software that seizes opportunities or targeted attacks, is known as network security.

Application security - aims to keep devices and software safe from harm. The data that an application is meant to safeguard may be accessible if it is compromised. Effective security starts at the design phase, long before a program or gadget is put into use. Data integrity and privacy are safeguarded during storage and transmission through the use of information security.

Operational security - covers the procedures and choices used to manage and safeguard data assets. the protocols that determine how and where users access networks, the permissions they have, and that determine how and where data may be stored or shared all fall under this umbrella.

Disaster recovery and business continuity define how an organization responds to a cyber-security incident or any other event that causes the loss of operations or data. Disaster recovery policies dictate how the organization restores its operations and information to return to the same operating capacity as before the event. Business continuity is the plan the organization falls back on while trying to operate without certain resources.

End-user education addresses the most unpredictable cyber-security factor: people. Anyone can accidentally introduce a virus to an otherwise secure system by failing to follow good security practices. Teaching users to delete suspicious email attachments, not plug in unidentified USB drives, and various other important lessons is vital for the security of any organization.

PART 2 NETWORK SECURITY

Network security is the practice of protecting computer networks and their components from unauthorized access, misuse, modification, or destruction. It involves implementing measures to prevent security breaches, detecting intrusions, and responding to security incidents. One massive example of Network security breaches is the NHS in the UK.

The National Health Service (NHS) in the UK is responsible for managing sensitive medical data and personal information of millions of patients. Unfortunately, there have been several data breaches within the NHS in recent years, which have resulted in the exposure of patient data and personal information.

Some examples of NHS data breaches include:

In 2017, the NHS suffered a major cyber-attack, which resulted in the loss of thousands of patient records. The attack was caused by a ransomware virus called WannaCry, which exploited a vulnerability in outdated Windows software.

In 2018, it was reported that NHS staff had inappropriately accessed the medical records of patients, with some staff members selling the information to third parties.

In 2019, a data breach at NHS Highland led to the exposure of the personal information of thousands of patients. The breach was caused by an email error, which resulted in sensitive information being sent to the wrong recipient.

And more recently, in 2020, it was reported that the NHS had inadvertently exposed the personal information of over 18,000 people who had been diagnosed with HIV. The data breach occurred when an email was sent to a group of individuals, and the email addresses of all recipients were visible to others.

These data breaches are concerning, as they can lead to a loss of trust in the NHS and the healthcare system as a whole. It is important for the NHS to take steps to prevent data breaches, such as implementing strong security measures and providing staff with appropriate training on data protection. Additionally, patients should be informed of any data breaches that occur, so that they can take steps to protect themselves from potential identity theft or other forms of fraud.

Fundamental concepts of Network Security include:

Confidentiality: Ensuring that information is only accessible to authorized users and is kept private from unauthorized users.

Integrity: Ensuring that information is not modified or altered by unauthorized users.

Availability: Ensuring that information and network resources are available to authorized users when needed.

Authentication: Verifying the identity of users or devices attempting to access the network or its resources.

Authorization: Granting or restricting access to network resources based on user or device credentials.

Encryption: Converting information into a form that can only be read by authorized users, using cryptographic algorithms.

Firewalls: Network security devices that monitor and control incoming and outgoing network traffic based on predetermined security rules.

Intrusion Detection Systems (IDS): Network security systems that detect and alert administrators to potential security breaches.

Virtual Private Networks (VPNs): Secure connections that allow remote users to access a private network over the public Internet.

Patch Management: Ensuring that network devices are updated with the latest security patches and software updates to prevent known vulnerabilities from being exploited.

These concepts and technologies are essential for maintaining a secure network and protecting against cyber threats. It is important to regularly review and update network security measures to stay ahead of evolving threats and vulnerabilities.

Hardening refers to securing a system by reducing its surface of vulnerability. Here are some important ways to harden a computer system or network:

- Keep all software up to date with the latest patches and security fixes. This includes the operating system, applications, firmware, etc.
- Remove unnecessary software, services, features, usernames and drives to minimize avenues of attack. Disable components that are not needed.

- Secure the configuration of the system by following the principle of least privilege. Disable default accounts and restrict permissions.

- Enable security features like antivirus, firewalls, intrusion detection/ prevention systems (IDS/IPS), data encryption etc.

- Use strong password policies and multi-factor authentication wherever possible to prevent unauthorized access.

- Restrict physical access to devices and isolate particularly sensitive systems and data.

- Implement the practice of regular backups to enable recovery in case of compromises or data loss due to hardware failure or malicious activity.

- Set up system logging and network monitoring solutions to detect anomalous activity and cyber threats early. Establish monitoring processes and alerting.

- Establish patch management and configuration change control workflows to maintain a consistent hardened state.

- Conduct vulnerability assessments and penetration tests to identify weaknesses and attack vectors that need to be secured.

- Provide cybersecurity training to employees regarding practices like password hygiene, identifying phishing, and reporting risks.

- Stay up to date on the latest threats and utilize threat intelligence to enhance defences proactively.

The goal of hardening is to eliminate as many security risks as possible and make the system highly resistant to cyber-attacks leveraging both technology and processes. It's an ongoing practice requiring regular audits and maintenance. Applications are secure and less vulnerable to attacks.

D ata encryption is the process of encoding information in such a way that only authorized parties can access it. Here are some key points about encrypting data:

Encryption converts readable data (called plaintext) into scrambled ciphertext that looks like random gibberish.

It uses cryptographic algorithms and keys to encrypt and decrypt the data. Common algorithms include AES, Blowfish, RC4, DES, and RSA.

The encryption keys are essential for decoding the data. Public key encryption uses a public and private key pair. A symmetric key uses the same key to encrypt and decrypt.

Encryption protects data privacy and integrity. It prevents unauthorised access to sensitive data stored on devices, networks, cloud services, etc.

Proper key management is critical. If keys are lost, stolen, or compromised, the encrypted data can become inaccessible.

Applications include encrypting files and hard drives, communications like email and instant messaging, passwords, blockchain transactions, website connections, and more.

Regulations often mandate encryption for personal data like healthcare records, financial information, PII, and confidential corporate data.

Benefits include information security, privacy, compliance, and shielding sensitive data from cybercriminals. However, it can impact system performance.

Encryption provides an important defence layer but must be combined with access controls, backups, endpoint security, and other measures for robust data protection.

D NS security refers to protecting the Domain Name System (DNS) from cyber threats like malware, phishing, and DDoS attacks. Here are some key ways to enhance DNS security:

Use DNS over HTTPS (DoH) or DNS over TLS (DoT) to encrypt DNS queries and prevent eavesdropping or manipulation of DNS traffic.

Enable DNSSEC on the DNS server to authenticate responses using digital signatures and prevent DNS cache poisoning.

Use a firewall or proxy to filter unwanted DNS traffic and detect anomalous activity like high volumes of queries.

Configure rate limiting on the DNS server to prevent excessive resource consumption from DDoS attacks.

Use solutions like Response Policy Zones (RPZ) to implement access controls and block requests to malicious domains.

Enable logging and monitoring to detect issues like spoofed DNS queries, unauthorized zone transfers, etc.

Ensure the DNS server is kept patched and up to date to mitigate vulnerabilities. Disable unnecessary services and ports.

Use DNS registrar locks to prevent unauthorized changes or transfers of DNS settings and records.

Implement multi-factor authentication and restrict admin access to prevent unauthorized configuration changes.

Separate public DNS servers from internal ones holding sensitive information. Use split-horizon DNS.

Educate employees on DNS-based threats like phishing and importance of keeping software updated.

Have a backup DNS server and recovery plan in case the primary server fails or is compromised.

Adopting these best practices will go a long way in securing your DNS infrastructure from modern threats.

Passwordless authentication

This is a method of verifying a user's identity without requiring them to enter a traditional password. Instead, it relies on alternative authentication factors, such as:

Biometrics: Using fingerprint scans, facial recognition, or other biometric data to confirm the user's identity.

One-Time Passwords (OTP): Sending a time-sensitive code to the user's registered device (via email, SMS, or a mobile app) for them to enter.

Authentication Tokens: Utilizing hardware tokens or mobile apps like Google Authenticator to generate codes for authentication.

Smart Cards: Employing physical smart cards or virtual smart card emulation on mobile devices.

FIDO2: Utilizing the FIDO2 standard, which enables secure passwordless authentication using public key cryptography.

Passwordless authentication is considered more secure than traditional password-based methods because it reduces the risk of password-related vulnerabilities, such as weak passwords or password reuse. It also offers a more user-friendly experience and can enhance security in various online services and applications.

Quantum cryptography

Quantum cryptography is a branch of cryptography that uses principles from quantum mechanics to secure communications. It is based on the fundamental properties of quantum mechanics, such as the uncertainty principle and the no-cloning theorem, to provide security features not achievable with classical cryptography. Quantum cryptography typically involves two main protocols:

Quantum Key Distribution (QKD): QKD allows two parties to generate a shared secret key over a quantum communication channel. The key is created using the properties of quantum entanglement and the behaviour of quantum particles. Any attempt to intercept or eavesdrop on the quantum communication would disrupt it, alerting the parties to the intrusion.

Quantum-Safe Cryptography: Quantum computers have the potential to break many commonly used cryptographic algorithms (e.g., RSA and ECC) due to their ability to efficiently solve certain mathematical problems. To prepare for this threat, researchers are developing quantum-resistant cryptographic algorithms, also known as post-quantum or quantum-safe cryptography.

Quantum cryptography offers the promise of secure communication channels that are theoretically immune to attacks by quantum computers. However, it is still an evolving field with practical challenges, and its widespread adoption is currently limited. Nevertheless, it represents a significant advancement in the quest for highly secure communication methods.

Mobile security Fundamentals

Mobile security is the practice of protecting mobile devices, their data, and the networks they access from unauthorized access, theft, and other cyber threats. Here are some fundamental aspects of mobile security:

Use a strong password: A strong password is the first line of defence against unauthorized access to your mobile device. Use a unique, complex password that includes a mix of uppercase and lowercase letters, numbers, and symbols.

Keep your device software up to date: Make sure you have the latest security updates and patches installed on your device. These updates often address security vulnerabilities that could be exploited by hackers.

Install security software: Install anti-malware and anti-virus software on your device to protect against malicious apps and other threats.

Be cautious of public Wi-Fi: Public Wi-Fi networks are often unsecured and can be used by hackers to intercept your data. Avoid accessing sensitive information on public Wi-Fi networks.

Use encryption: Use encryption to protect your data from prying eyes. Encryption technology makes it difficult for hackers to access and read your data.

Disable Bluetooth and NFC when not in use: Bluetooth and NFC can be used to transfer files and connect to devices.

U sing public Wi-Fi networks can be convenient, but it also poses security risks. Here are some tips to help protect your privacy and security when using public Wi-Fi:

Avoid accessing sensitive information: Try to avoid accessing sensitive information, such as online banking, shopping, or entering passwords, while using public Wi-Fi.

Use a VPN: A virtual private network (VPN) can help protect your online activity and data by encrypting your internet connection. There are many VPN services available, both free and paid.

Check the network name: Make sure you are connecting to the correct public Wi-Fi network. Hackers can create fake networks with similar names to lure people into connecting to them.

Turn off sharing: Disable file sharing on your device to prevent others from accessing your files and folders.

Keep your device updated: Make sure your device's operating system and apps are up to date with the latest security patches.

Use HTTPS: Look for websites that use HTTPS encryption, which encrypts your communication with the website, making it more difficult for anyone to intercept your data.

Use two-factor authentication: Use two-factor authentication whenever possible to add an extra layer of security to your online accounts.

By following these tips, you can help protect your privacy and security when using public Wi-Fi networks.

IoT Security Measures

IoT security refers to the measures and practices implemented to protect internet-connected devices and systems from unauthorized access, misuse, modification, and theft of data. As more and more devices become connected to the internet, the need for IoT security becomes increasingly important to ensure the safety and privacy of individuals and organizations. Here are key aspects of IoT security:

Authentication and authorization: Devices and users should be properly authenticated and authorized before they are granted access to the network or system.

Encryption: Data transmitted between devices should be encrypted to prevent interception and manipulation.

Network segmentation: IoT devices should be segmented into different networks to limit the damage that can be done in case of a security breach.

Firmware updates: Devices should be kept up to date with the latest firmware updates to patch any security vulnerabilities.

Physical security: Physical access to devices should be restricted to prevent theft or unauthorized tampering.

User education: Users should be educated on safe IoT practices and how to recognize and respond to security threats.

Implementing these measures and staying up to date with the latest IoT security best practices can help ensure the security of IoT devices and systems.

What does Zero trust mean in Cybersecurity? Zero trust is a cybersecurity framework that operates under the principle of "never trust, always verify". The key ideas behind zero trust are:

Assume breach - Always assume there may be a breach and do not automatically trust anything inside or outside the network perimeter.

Least privilege access - Only grant access to resources on a need-to-know basis. Access should be tightly controlled and monitored.

Strict identity verification - Rigorously verify the identity of every user, device, and application before granting access to resources.

Micro-segmentation - Divide the network into small segments and limit communication between segments. This helps limit lateral movement in the event of a breach.

Continuous monitoring - Continuously monitor and log all activity to detect threats as early as possible.

Multi-factor authentication - Require additional factors like one-time passwords or biometric factors for user authentication.

Endpoint security - Secure endpoints like mobiles and laptops, as they are highly vulnerable.

So, in summary, zero trust minimizes risk by eliminating implicit trust and continuously validating every stage of digital interactions. The goal is to evolve security from a perimeter-based approach to one that is identity and context-aware.

Endpoint security Fundamentals

Endpoint security is the practice of securing the various endpoints, or devices, which are connected to a network. Endpoints can include desktops, laptops, servers, mobile devices, and other devices that have access to a network.

Here are some fundamental concepts of endpoint security:

Threat Prevention: Endpoint security solutions provide real-time protection against various threats such as malware, ransomware, viruses, and phishing attacks. Endpoint security solutions use various techniques such as signature-based detection, behavioural analysis, and machine learning to identify and prevent threats.

Endpoint Detection and Response (EDR): EDR is a type of endpoint security solution that helps to detect and respond to advanced threats that may have evaded other security measures. EDR solutions monitor endpoints for suspicious activity and provide alerts to security teams.

Patch Management: Patch management is the process of ensuring that all endpoints are updated with the latest security patches and software updates. Endpoint security solutions can automate this process, ensuring that all endpoints are updated in a timely manner.

Access Control: Endpoint security solutions can enforce access control policies, ensuring that only authorized users and devices can access sensitive data and resources.

Data Encryption: Endpoint security solutions can also encrypt sensitive data stored on endpoints. Encryption ensures that even if a device is lost or stolen, the data stored on it remains secure.

Remote Wipe: Endpoint security solutions can also enable security teams to remotely wipe data from lost or stolen devices, ensuring that sensitive data does not fall into the wrong hands.

In summary, Endpoint security is a critical component of any organization's overall security strategy. By implementing endpoint security solutions, organizations can protect their endpoints against various threats and ensure that sensitive data remains secure.

An air-gapped network

This term refers to a computer network that is physically or logically separated from untrusted networks, such as the Internet or other external networks. This isolation is achieved by ensuring that there are no physical or network connections between the air-gapped network and the outside world.

Airgapped networks are typically employed in highly secure environments where data confidentiality and integrity are paramount. Common examples include military networks, government agencies, financial institutions, research laboratories, and critical infrastructure systems.

The primary purpose of using an air-gapped network is to minimize the risk of unauthorized access, data breaches, and malware infections that may result from network connectivity. By isolating the network, it becomes significantly more challenging for attackers to inflict connections like network cables, wireless access points, or other communication channels linking the isolated network to the outside world.

Data transfer methods: Since direct network connections are absent, data transfer between air-gapped networks and external systems must rely on alternative methods. This can include the use of removable media (such as USB drives), physically transporting storage devices, or employing dedicated secure systems for data exchange.

Security protocols: Airgapped networks employ strict security protocols to ensure the integrity and confidentiality of data. This includes stringent access controls, robust authentication mechanisms, encryption techniques, and monitoring systems to detect any unauthorized attempts to breach the network.

Operational challenges: Operating an air-gapped network comes with various challenges. For instance, software updates and patches must be manually applied, as automatic updates are not feasible. Additionally, information exchange between the airgapped network and external systems requires careful planning and security measures to prevent potential threats.

Human factor: While airgapped networks provide a high level of security, the human factor remains a significant vulnerability. Social engineering attacks or physical access to the network by unauthorized individuals can still compromise the security of the isolated environment.

It is important to note that even with the strongest security measures, no network is entirely immune to attacks. Sophisticated adversaries have developed techniques like side-channel attacks, covert channels, or even using removable media as an attack vector to bypass airgap security. Therefore, organizations must continually assess and update their security measures to mitigate potential risks effectively.

Overall, airgapped networks play a crucial role in safeguarding sensitive information and critical systems from cyber threats by physically isolating them from untrusted networks, filtrate or exfiltrate sensitive information.

Bitcoin security is an important aspect of the popular cryptocurrency since 2009. Here are some key points to consider regarding Bitcoin security:

Blockchain Technology: Bitcoin operates on a decentralized ledger called the blockchain. It is a distributed network of computers (nodes) that work together to validate and record transactions. The blockchain's transparency and immutability contribute to the security of Bitcoin.

Private Keys: Bitcoin uses public-key cryptography, where users have a pair of cryptographic keys: a public key and a private key. The private key is essential for accessing and managing Bitcoin holdings. It is crucial to keep your private keys secure and never share them with anyone, as anyone with access to your private key can control your Bitcoin.

Wallet Security: Bitcoin wallets are software or hardware devices used to store and manage Bitcoin. Wallets come in various forms, including software wallets (desktop, mobile, web-based) and hardware wallets (physical devices). It is important to choose a reputable wallet provider and ensure your wallet is secure by enabling features like two-factor authentication (2FA) and strong passwords.

Cold Storage: Cold storage refers to storing Bitcoin offline, away from internet-connected devices. Cold storage methods include hardware wallets, paper wallets (printed copies of private keys), and other offline storage solutions. Cold storage provides a high level of security as it is less susceptible to hacking or online attacks.

Secure Exchanges: Bitcoin can be bought, sold, and traded on cryptocurrency exchanges. When using an exchange, it is crucial to choose a reputable and secure platform with robust security measures, such as two-factor authentication, withdrawal whitelisting, and cold storage for funds.

Avoiding Phishing and Scams: Bitcoin users should be cautious of phishing attempts, scams, and fraudulent websites. Always double-check URLs, enable browser security features, and be wary of unsolicited requests for personal information or Bitcoin transfers.

Network Consensus: Bitcoin's security is also maintained through network consensus. Miners, who use computational power to validate transactions and add them to the blockchain, play a vital role in securing the network. The consensus mechanism (Proof-of-Work) ensures that the majority of miners are honest and prevents malicious actors from controlling the network.

Software Updates: Keeping your Bitcoin wallet software and other relevant software up to date is essential. Developers regularly release updates to fix security vulnerabilities and improve overall security.

While Bitcoin offers robust security measures, it is important for individual users to be responsible and follow best practices to protect their holdings.

PART 3 - APPLICATION SECURITY

Application security refers to the practice of securing software applications from malicious attacks, vulnerabilities, and threats. Application security is important because software applications are increasingly becoming the target of attacks due to the proliferation of technology, and the ever-increasing amount of sensitive data that is stored in these applications.

Here are some fundamental principles of application security:

Threat Modelling: Threat modelling is the process of identifying potential threats to an application and determining how to mitigate them. This process is important because it helps developers to understand how an attacker might exploit a vulnerability in the application and develop effective security controls to mitigate that risk.

Secure coding practices: Secure coding practices involve the use of coding techniques that make software less vulnerable to attacks. This includes principles like input validation, output encoding, and error handling.

Access control: Access control is the process of ensuring that only authorized users can access an application. This includes implementing user authentication and authorization and restricting access to sensitive data.

Encryption: Encryption is the process of converting data into a coded form that cannot easily be read by unauthorized individuals. This is important in applications that store sensitive data, such as credit card numbers, personal information, or medical records.

Regular testing and updates: Regular testing and updates are essential to maintaining application security. Developers should regularly test applications for vulnerabilities and update them to patch any known vulnerabilities.

Security training: Security training is an essential aspect of application security. All developers, testers, and administrators who work with the application should receive regular training on security best practices and emerging threats.

PART 3.1 OPERATIONAL SECURITY

Operational security (OPSEC) is the process of identifying and protecting critical information from being exploited by adversaries. It is a fundamental principle of information security and is essential to protect individuals, organizations, and nations from threats to their security.

Here are some fundamental principles of operational security:

Identify Critical Information: Identify and classify the critical information that needs protection. This could include personally identifiable information (PII), financial information, intellectual property, or sensitive government information.

Conduct Risk Assessments: Conduct risk assessments to identify potential threats and vulnerabilities to the critical information. This includes identifying the adversaries who could exploit the information, their motives, and their methods.

Develop Countermeasures: Develop countermeasures to mitigate the identified risks. This could include developing security policies, implementing access controls, encryption, or physical security measures.

Train Employees: Train employees on the importance of operational security and how to implement it. This includes educating employees on how to identify and protect critical information, how to report security incidents, and how to follow security policies and procedures.

Monitor and Evaluate: Monitor and evaluate the effectiveness of the operational security program. This includes regularly reviewing security policies and procedures, testing security controls, and conducting security audits.

PART 3.2 - DISASTER RECOVERY AND BUSINESS CONTINUITY PLANNING

Disaster recovery and business continuity planning are essential components of a company's overall risk management strategy. These plans help ensure that critical business functions can continue in the event of a disaster or unexpected interruption.

Here are some fundamental steps to consider when developing a disaster recovery/business continuity plan:

Risk assessment: Identify potential risks and vulnerabilities to your organization, such as natural disasters, cyberattacks, power outages, etc.

Business impact analysis: Determine the potential impact of each risk on your organization, such as financial losses, reputational damage, operational disruptions, etc.

Develop a plan: Based on the risk assessment and business impact analysis, develop a comprehensive plan to mitigate the potential impacts of each risk.

Communication: Ensure that all relevant stakeholders are aware of the disaster recovery/business continuity plan and their roles and responsibilities during an emergency.

Testing: Regularly test the plan to ensure that it is effective and up to date. This includes tabletop exercises, simulations, and actual drills.

Maintenance: Regularly review and update the plan to reflect changes in the organization, technology, and the environment.

Remember that disaster recovery and business continuity planning is an ongoing process. It requires regular updates and testing to ensure that the plan remains effective and relevant to the organization's needs.

Cybersecurity is an essential part of modern technology use. With the rise of digital devices and online communication, it is crucial for end-users to understand the basics of cybersecurity to protect themselves and their information from cyber threats.

Here are some essential topics:

Password security: Users should know how to create strong passwords and how to protect them. They should never reuse passwords across multiple accounts, and they should change their passwords regularly.

Phishing: Users should know how to recognize and avoid phishing scams, which are fraudulent emails or messages designed to trick people into providing personal information or login credentials.

Social engineering: Users should understand the basics of social engineering tactics, such as pretexting, baiting, and tailgating, and how to avoid falling victim to them.

Malware: Users should be aware of several types of malware, such as viruses, Trojans, and ransomware, and how to avoid downloading and installing malicious software.

Mobile device security: Users should know how to secure their mobile devices, such as smartphones and tablets, with strong passwords or biometric authentication, and how to avoid downloading apps from untrusted sources.

Safe browsing practices: Users should understand how to browse the internet safely, including how to recognize and avoid malicious websites, and how to use browser extensions and ad-blockers to protect themselves from online threats.

Data backup: Users should understand the importance of data backup, and how to create backups of important files and data to protect against data loss due to cyberattacks or system failures.

Software updates: Users should know the importance of keeping their software up to date, including operating systems, applications, and antivirus software, to protect against known security vulnerabilities.

Two-factor authentication: Users should understand the benefits of two factor authentication, which requires a second form of authentication, such as a fingerprint or a text message code, in addition to a password, to access an account.

Privacy settings: Users should know how to adjust privacy settings on their devices and online accounts to control what information is shared and who can access it. Overall, these topics are just a few essential cybersecurity basics that end users should understand to protect themselves and their information from cyber threats. Ongoing education and awareness are critical to staying safe in today's digital age.

Cloud security refers to the set of policies, technologies, and controls designed to protect the data, applications, and infrastructure of cloud computing services from cyber threats and attacks.

CYBERSECURITY FUNDAMENTALS EXPLAINED

Here are some fundamental concepts related to cloud security:

Shared responsibility model: The shared responsibility model is a security framework that outlines the responsibilities of a cloud service provider (CSP) and its customers in securing and protecting data and applications in the cloud. The model defines a clear separation of security responsibilities between the CSP and its customers, ensuring that both parties are accountable for different aspects of security.

Under the shared responsibility model, the CSP is responsible for the security of the cloud infrastructure, including the physical data centres, servers, storage, and network hardware. The CSP also ensures the availability and accessibility of the cloud services, as well as the security of the underlying software, including the operating systems and application frameworks.

On the other hand, the customers are responsible for securing their data and applications within the cloud environment. This includes securing their user access controls, configurations, network traffic, and encryption of sensitive data. Customers are also responsible for managing their user accounts and ensuring that they comply with industry regulations and standards.

The shared responsibility model provides a clear framework for both the CSP and customers to understand their respective security responsibilities. By defining the roles and responsibilities of each party, the model helps ensure that both parties work together to maintain a secure and compliant cloud environment. This helps to reduce the risk of security breaches, data loss, and other security incidents that could negatively impact businesses and their customers.

Encryption: Cloud encryption refers to the process of encrypting data before it is stored in a cloud computing environment. Cloud encryption is used to protect sensitive data such as financial information, personal data, and confidential business information from unauthorized access or theft.

The encryption process involves transforming the data into an unreadable format that can only be decrypted with the correct key or password. Cloud encryption can be implemented at different layers of the cloud computing stack, including the application, database, and storage layers.

There are several types of cloud encryption, including symmetric encryption, asymmetric encryption, and homomorphic encryption. Symmetric encryption uses the same key for both encryption and decryption, while asymmetric encryption uses different keys for encryption and decryption. Homomorphic encryption is a more complex form of encryption that allows computations to be performed on encrypted data without decrypting it first.

Cloud encryption can be implemented by cloud service providers, or it can be implemented by organizations using cloud services to protect their data. When implementing cloud encryption, it is important to consider factors such as key management, access control, and compliance with regulatory requirements. Cloud providers offer encryption for data at rest and data in transit.

Identity and access management (IAM): Identity and Access Management (IAM) is a set of processes, policies, and technologies used to manage and secure access to digital resources within an organization. IAM enables the creation, management, and maintenance of digital identities and access rights across different systems and applications.

IAM typically involves four main components:

Identification: The process of establishing the identity of a user or entity, usually by verifying a username and password, or through multi-factor authentication methods.

Authentication: The process of verifying the identity of a user or entity, usually through a set of credentials (such as a password, smart card, or biometric data).

Authorization: The process of granting or denying access to specific resources or actions based on a user's identity and level of access.

Accountability: The process of tracking and auditing access to resources and actions and ensuring compliance with policies and regulations.

IAM solutions may include directory services, access management tools, identity governance and administration (IGA) tools, and privileged access management (PAM) solutions. IAM is essential for maintaining the security and integrity of an organization's digital assets and protecting against data breaches and cyberattacks.

Multi-factor authentication (MFA): Multi-factor authentication (MFA) is a security mechanism that requires users to provide multiple forms of identification to verify their identity before they can access a system, application, or data. This approach enhances security by adding an additional layer of protection beyond just a username and password.

MFA typically involves the use of at least two of the following types of authentication factors:

Something you know: This includes a password, passphrase, or personal identification number (PIN).

Something you have: This includes a physical device like a smart card, token, or a mobile device that generates a one-time code.

Something you are: This includes biometric identification such as fingerprint or face recognition.

MFA has become increasingly important in today's digital world where cyber threats and data breaches are on the rise. It can help protect against attacks that involve stealing or guessing passwords, as well as other forms of identity theft. By requiring multiple forms of identification, MFA makes it much harder for attackers to impersonate legitimate users and gain unauthorized access to systems or data.

Security monitoring and logging:

Security monitoring and logging are critical components of any cloud computing security strategy. These practices involve collecting and analysing data from various sources to detect and respond to security incidents and potential threats. Here are some key considerations for security monitoring and logging in cloud computing:

Understand your cloud service provider's (CSP) security monitoring and logging capabilities: Different CSPs may offer different levels of monitoring and logging capabilities. It is important to understand what your CSP offers and whether it meets your organization's needs.

Establish a comprehensive logging policy: A logging policy should define what data is collected, how it is collected, where it is stored, and how long it is retained. It should also define access controls and audit requirements.

Monitor network traffic and activity logs: Network traffic logs can help detect anomalies or suspicious behaviour on the network, such as unusual traffic patterns or unauthorized access attempts. Activity logs can help track user behaviour, system changes, and application activity.

Utilize security information and event management (SIEM) tools: SIEM tools can help collect and analyse data from various sources, such as network traffic logs and activity logs, to detect security incidents and potential threats.

Implement automated alerts and response mechanisms: Automated alerts can notify security teams of potential threats or incidents in real-time, allowing for quick response and remediation. Automated response mechanisms, such as automated blocking or quarantining of malicious traffic, can also help prevent or mitigate security incidents.

Conduct regular security audits: Regular security audits can help identify vulnerabilities and gaps in your security monitoring and logging practices and ensure compliance with industry standards and regulations.

Overall, security monitoring and logging are critical for maintaining the security and integrity of cloud computing environments. By implementing these practices, organizations can detect and respond to security incidents in a timely manner and improve their overall security posture.

· · · ·

DISASTER RECOVERY AND business continuity: Disaster recovery and business continuity planning are essential components of a company's overall risk management strategy. These plans help ensure that critical business functions can continue in the event of a disaster or unexpected interruption.

Here are some fundamental steps to consider when developing a disaster recovery/business continuity plan:

Risk assessment: Identify potential risks and vulnerabilities to your organization, such as natural disasters, cyberattacks, power outages, etc.

Business impact analysis: Determine the potential impact of each risk on your organization, such as financial losses, reputational damage, operational disruptions, etc.

Develop a plan: Based on the risk assessment and business impact analysis, develop a comprehensive plan to mitigate the potential impacts of each risk.

Communication: Ensure that all relevant stakeholders are aware of the disaster recovery/business continuity plan and their roles and responsibilities during an emergency.

Testing: Regularly test the plan to ensure that it is effective and up to date. This includes tabletop exercises, simulations, and actual drills.

Maintenance: Regularly review and update the plan to reflect changes in the organization, technology, and the environment.

Remember that disaster recovery and business continuity planning is an ongoing process. It requires regular updates and testing to ensure that the plan remains effective and relevant to the organization's needs.

Compliance: Compliance in cloud computing refers to the adherence of cloud computing services and solutions to various regulatory and legal requirements. Compliance can include a range of measures, such as data protection, data privacy, security, and transparency.

Cloud computing providers are often subject to regulations such as the General Data Protection Regulation (GDPR) in the European Union or the Health Insurance Portability and Accountability Act (HIPAA) in the United States. These regulations require cloud providers to implement certain security and privacy controls to protect the data stored and processed in the cloud.

To ensure compliance, cloud providers may need to conduct regular audits and assessments to identify any vulnerabilities and areas for improvement. They may also need to implement specific technical and organizational measures to ensure data protection and privacy, such as encryption, access controls, and data segregation. Additionally, compliance requirements may differ depending on the type of cloud deployment model used, whether it is a public, private, or hybrid cloud. For example, a private cloud may have more stringent security and privacy requirements since it is typically used by a single organization, while a public cloud may need to adhere to regulations that are more universally applicable.

Overall, compliance in cloud computing is crucial to protect sensitive data and maintain the trust of customers who rely on cloud services for their business operations.

Biometric security refers to using unique biological or behavioural characteristics to authenticate and verify the identity of individuals. It offers a more secure and convenient alternative to traditional security methods like passwords or identification cards. Biometric systems capture and analyse specific traits such as fingerprints, iris patterns, voiceprints, facial features, or even behavioural patterns like typing rhythm or gait.

Here are some key aspects of biometric security:

Biometric Modalities: Biometric systems use different modalities to capture and analyse biometric traits. Some common modalities include:

Fingerprint recognition: Analysing the unique patterns on a person's fingertips.

Iris recognition: Examining the intricate patterns in the iris of the eye.

Facial recognition: Analysing the unique facial features and measurements.

Voice recognition: Analysing the distinctive characteristics of an individual's voice.

Palmprint recognition: Examining the patterns on a person's palm.

Behavioural biometrics: Analysing patterns in an individual's behaviour, such as typing rhythm or gait.

Enrolment: During enrolment, a user's biometric information is captured and stored in a secure database. This process involves scanning or capturing the relevant biometric trait using specialized devices like fingerprint scanners, iris scanners, cameras, or microphones.

Template Creation: Once the biometric information is captured, it is converted into a digital template. The template contains specific features or characteristics unique to the individual but does not store the complete biometric data. It is typically a mathematical representation or hash of the original biometric trait.

Matching and Verification: When a user attempts to gain access to a system or facility, the biometric system compares the presented biometric sample with the stored template. If the system finds a match within an acceptable threshold, the individual's identity is verified, and access is granted. This process is known as one-to-one matching or verification.

Identification: In some cases, the biometric system may need to identify an individual from a large database without prior knowledge of their identity. This process is known as one-to-many matching or identification. It involves comparing the presented biometric sample against templates of all enrolled individuals to find a potential match.

Security and Privacy: Biometric data is sensitive and must be securely stored and protected to prevent unauthorised access. Encryption techniques and secure storage systems are employed to safeguard biometric templates and prevent their misuse.

Advantages and Limitations: Biometric security offers several advantages, such as increased security, convenience, and the uniqueness of biometric traits. However, it is fallible, and there are limitations to consider, such as potential privacy concerns, the possibility of false positives or false negatives, and the need for backup authentication methods in case of biometric failure.

Biometric security systems are widely used in various domains, including access control systems, mobile devices, banking and financial systems, border control, and law enforcement. They continue to evolve and improve as technology advances, offering enhanced security and user experience.

PART 4 - INFORMATION SECURITY

Information security is slightly different to Cybersecurity and refers to the protection of digital and non-digital information from unauthorized access, use, disclosure, disruption, modification, or destruction. The following are some of the fundamental concepts and principles of information security:

Confidentiality: Ensuring that information is only accessible to authorized individuals and entities.

Integrity: Maintaining the accuracy, completeness, and consistency of information over its entire lifecycle.

Availability: Ensuring that information and the systems used to access it are always available when needed.

Authentication: Verifying the identity of users, systems, and devices to ensure that they are authorized to access the information.

Authorization: Determining what resources and actions users are allowed to access based on their roles and permissions.

Accountability: Holding users and systems responsible for their actions and ensuring that they can be traced back to their source.

Non-repudiation: Ensuring that the origin and authenticity of information cannot be denied by the sender.

Risk management: Risk management refers to the process of identifying, assessing, and prioritizing risks, and then taking steps to minimize, monitor, and control those risks. Risk management is an essential practice for organizations of all sizes and types, as it helps them to identify potential threats to their operations and develop strategies for mitigating those threats.

The risk management process typically involves the following steps:

Risk identification: Identifying potential risks that could affect an organization.

Risk assessment: Evaluating the likelihood and potential impact of each identified risk.

Risk prioritization: Ranking risks based on their severity and likelihood of occurrence.

Risk mitigation: Developing strategies to reduce the likelihood or impact of identified risks.

Risk monitoring: Continuously monitoring risks and adjusting mitigation strategies as needed.

Risk communication: Communicating risk information to stakeholders, including employees, customers, and investors.

Effective risk management can help organizations avoid financial losses, protect their reputation, and ensure compliance with laws and regulations. It is an ongoing process that requires ongoing vigilance and attention to changing risks and circumstances.

Security policies: An information security policy is a set of guidelines, rules, and procedures that define how an organization manages, protects, and secures its information assets. The policy aims to ensure the confidentiality, integrity, and availability of information by setting out the standards, procedures, and practices that need to be followed to safeguard information. A comprehensive information security policy typically covers several areas, including:

Access control: policies and procedures to manage user access to information resources.

Data protection: policies and procedures to secure data at rest and in transit.

Incident management: policies and procedures to manage security incidents and minimize the impact of security breaches.

Network security: policies and procedures to secure the organization's network infrastructure.

Physical security: policies and procedures to secure the organization's physical assets, such as buildings, servers, and other equipment.

Risk management: policies and procedures to assess and manage security risks.

Security awareness and training: policies and procedures to educate employees about information security best practices.

Third-party management: policies and procedures to manage third-party vendors and contractors that have access to the organization's information assets.

Creating and implementing an effective information security policy requires a collaborative effort between different departments, such as IT, legal, human resources, and senior management. The policy should be regularly reviewed and updated to reflect changes in the threat landscape and the organization's evolving security needs.

Security awareness: Educating users about the importance of information security and their role in protecting it.

These concepts and principles are essential for designing, implementing, and maintaining effective information security practices in organizations.

4.1 Storage security

Here are some best practices for securing data storage systems and infrastructure:

Use encryption to protect data at rest and in transit. Manage keys properly and use standards like AES-256.

Utilize access controls like file permissions, multi-factor authentication, VLANs, and firewall rules to restrict access.

Implement the principle of least privilege - only allow the minimum access needed. Disable default accounts.

Regularly patch, update, and harden operating systems, databases, applications, and hardware firmware.

Utilize intrusion detection and data loss prevention solutions to monitor for unauthorized activity.

Establish backup and disaster recovery systems for crucial data. Test backups regularly.

Physically secure storage hardware, servers, and media in locked facilities with controlled access.

Dispose of old or decommissioned hardware securely by doing wipe disks, destroying drives, etc.

Maintain logs of access and changes for auditing purposes. Use unique identifiers for accessing systems.

Train personnel in secure practices like proper password management, recognizing social engineering, and reporting risks.

Develop incident response plans for response in case of a data breach, loss or exposure.

Assess storage infrastructure security regularly via audits, penetration tests, and risk evaluations.

Monitor emerging threats and utilize threat intelligence to enhance defences proactively.

Following these best practices reduces the risk of unauthorized access, cyberattacks, data leaks, and system exploitation.

E mail security refers to the measures taken to protect email messages from unauthorized access, interception, and compromise. Email security is important because email is often used to transmit sensitive information such as personal data, financial information, and confidential business communication.

Here are some common email security measures:

Strong passwords: Use strong passwords that are difficult to guess and change them regularly.

Encryption: Use encryption to protect the content of email messages from interception by unauthorized parties. Encryption can be done at various levels, such as end-to-end encryption or transport-layer encryption.

Anti-virus and anti-malware software: Use anti-virus and anti-malware software to scan email attachments and detect and remove any malicious code.

Two-factor authentication: Enable two-factor authentication to add an extra layer of security to your email account. This requires a second factor such as a code sent to your phone, in addition to your password.

Phishing protection: Be aware of phishing attacks, which are attempts to trick you into revealing sensitive information. Use tools such as spam filters and email scanners to detect and block phishing emails.

User awareness: Educate users about email security best practices, such as not clicking on suspicious links or downloading attachments from unknown sources.

Overall, email security is an ongoing process that requires a combination of technical measures and user awareness. By following best practices and using the right tools, you can protect your email communication from unauthorized access and compromise.

Here are some key elements and best practices for establishing strong perimeter security:

Physical barriers - Fences, walls, vehicle barriers, and controlled entry points to deter and prevent unauthorized physical access.

Access controls - Security guards, authentication mechanisms, badge access systems, biometrics, and visitor management procedures.

Surveillance systems - Security cameras, video surveillance, and intrusion detection systems to monitor the premises.

Lighting - Adequate lighting of facility exteriors and entrances to eliminate blind spots and deter criminal activity.

Secure ingresses/egresses - Limited entry/exit points, crash-rated vehicle barriers, sally ports, mantraps, and double-door interlocks.

Employee/visitor screening - Reception desks, metal detectors, x-ray screening, bag checks, and identification verification.

Signage - Warning signs, property boundary markings and notices to create visibility and awareness.

Layered security - Multiple, integrated physical controls for defence-in-depth rather than relying on single measures.

Regular testing - Audits and penetration testing to check for vulnerabilities and address gaps in controls.

Maintenance - Timely repair of broken physical barriers, landscape grooming, appropriate technology upgrades.

Cybersecurity monitoring - Networking monitoring, intrusion detection systems, and endpoint protections.

Effective perimeter security balances access control, surveillance, and layered physical reinforcements tailored to facility size, function, assets, threats, and vulnerabilities.

PART 5 - CYBERSECURITY TECHNOLOGIES AND BEST PRACTICES

Cybersecurity is a critical concern for organizations of all sizes, and there are a variety of technologies and best practices that can help mitigate cyber risks. Here are some key technologies and best practices in cybersecurity:

Technologies:

A Firewall: A firewall is a network security device or software that monitors, and filters incoming and outgoing network traffic based on predefined security rules.

Intrusion Detection System (IDS) and Intrusion Prevention System (IPS): An IDS monitors network traffic for suspicious activity and alerts security personnel when it detects potential intrusions. An IPS goes a step further by automatically blocking suspicious activity.

Virtual Private Network (VPN): A VPN allows users to securely access a private network over the internet. It encrypts data in transit and ensures confidentiality and integrity.

Encryption: Encryption is the process of converting plain text into code, making it unreadable without the right key. It can be used to protect data at rest (stored data) and data in transit (data moving over a network).

Two-factor Authentication (2FA): 2FA adds an extra layer of security to the login process by requiring users to provide two forms of authentication (e.g., a password and a code sent to their phone).

Best Practices: Employee Education and Training: One of the best practices for cybersecurity is to educate employees on how to identify and avoid cyber threats. Regular training sessions and awareness programs can help employees stay vigilant against phishing attacks, malware, and other cyber threats.

Regular Security Updates: Keeping software, operating systems, and other technology up to date with the latest security patches is crucial for minimizing vulnerabilities that can be exploited by cybercriminals.

Access Control: Organizations should implement access controls that limit employee access to sensitive data and systems. This includes user authentication, role-based access control, and least privilege access.

Data Backup and Disaster Recovery: Regular data backups and disaster recovery planning can help organizations quickly recover from cyber-attacks and minimize the impact of data breaches.

Incident Response Plan: A well-defined incident response plan is crucial for quickly identifying and responding to cyber threats. It should include steps for containing the threat, assessing the damage, and restoring normal operations.

End user education: Here are some best practices for educating end users on cybersecurity:

Hold regular cybersecurity training sessions to teach employees policies, threats, safe practices, and how to report risks. Make training mandatory.

Send simulated phishing and ransomware emails to test readiness. Use results to further educate on threats.

Ensure training covers secure password management, email safety, social engineering risks, Wi-Fi use, safe web browsing, mobile security, etc.

Tailor training to different user roles like executives who face greater risk. Consider job-specific real-world examples.

Utilize engaging training methods like videos, visual aids, quizzes, and hands-on demos instead of just presentations.

Test comprehension after training by having users affirm understanding of policies and enumerate threats.

Send helpful cybersecurity tips regularly through email, blogs, posters, and internal communications.

Foster a collaborative culture where users are encouraged to discuss concerns, ask questions, and propose improvements.

Incentivize secure behaviour through gamification, rewards programs, and recognition of security-minded employees.

Enforce accountability by enacting consequences for violations of policies and repeat offenders.

Update training content frequently to cover new methods used by attackers and evolving threats.

Combined with technology controls, comprehensive end user education is key to building a strong human firewall and cyber resilience. It's an ongoing process requiring continuous engagement.

PART 6 – SECURITY INFORMATION AND EVENT MANAGEMENT (SIEM)

Security Information and Event Management (SIEM) is a software solution that enables organizations to collect and analyse security-related data from various sources across their network infrastructure such as one of the more commonly used called "Splunk." SIEM solutions integrate data from various sources, including security devices, servers, applications, and endpoints, and use advanced analytics techniques to identify and respond to security incidents.

SIEM solutions typically provide real-time monitoring and alerts for security events, allowing security analysts to quickly detect and respond to security incidents. They can also provide historical analysis of security events, which can be used for forensic investigations or compliance reporting.

Some key features of SIEM solutions include:

Log Collection: SIEM solutions collect logs from various sources across the network, including firewalls, intrusion detection systems (IDS), intrusion prevention systems (IPS), and other security devices.

Correlation: SIEM solutions correlate events from multiple sources to identify patterns and potential security incidents.

Alerting: SIEM solutions can generate alerts for security incidents, which can be sent to security analysts or other stakeholders.

Reporting: SIEM solutions can generate reports on security events, which can be used for compliance reporting, audit trails, or forensic investigations.

Dashboard: SIEM solutions can provide a dashboard that displays real-time information on security events, alerts, and other key metrics.

SIEM solutions play a crucial role in the overall security posture of an organization by providing a centralized view of security events across the network. They can help organizations detect and respond to security incidents quickly and effectively, reducing the impact of security breaches and minimizing the risk of data loss or theft.

PART 7 – COMMON AND NOT SO COMMON ATTACKS AND THREATS

Examples of some of The Biggest Cybersecurity attacks

There have been many notable cybersecurity attacks throughout history, but here are some of the biggest and most damaging ones:

Equifax: In 2017, Equifax, a credit reporting agency, suffered a massive data breach that exposed the personal information of over 147 million people, including names, social security numbers, birth dates, and more.

Yahoo: Yahoo suffered multiple data breaches in 2013 and 2014 that compromised the personal information of all of its three billion user accounts, including names, email addresses, birth dates, and security questions and answers.

Target: In 2013, Target experienced a data breach that exposed the personal and financial information of over 110 million customers, including credit and debit card numbers, names, addresses, and phone numbers.

Sony Pictures: In 2014, Sony Pictures experienced a cyber-attack that resulted in the theft and release of a large amount of confidential and sensitive data, including emails, employee data, financial information, and unreleased movies.

WannaCry: In 2017, WannaCry ransomware spread rapidly across the globe, infecting hundreds of thousands of computers in over 150 countries, and causing significant disruptions to critical infrastructure, including healthcare, transportation, and telecommunications.

NotPetya: In 2017, NotPetya, a destructive malware attack, caused significant damage to numerous companies, particularly in Ukraine, where it disrupted critical infrastructure, including banks, energy companies, and transportation systems.

SolarWinds: More recently, in 2020, a massive cyber-attack on SolarWinds, a network management software company, resulted in the compromise of numerous government and private sector organizations worldwide, including several US government agencies.

These are just a few examples of some of the biggest cybersecurity attacks in recent history. It is important to note that as technology evolves, so do the threats and risks associated with it, and it is crucial for individuals and organizations to take proactive measures to protect themselves from potential cyber threats.

There are several common cyber threats that individuals and organizations should be aware of, including:

• • • •

PHISHING: PHISHING is a technique used by cybercriminals to trick individuals into providing sensitive information, such as login credentials, social security numbers, or credit card information. This is usually done through a fake email or website that looks legitimate.

Malware: Malware is any software designed to damage or exploit computer systems. It can come in various forms such as viruses, worms, Trojans, and spyware. Malware can be used to steal sensitive information, take control of systems, or cause damage to devices.

Ransomware: Ransomware is a type of malware that encrypts a victim's files and demands a ransom payment in exchange for the decryption key. This is a particularly insidious type of attack, as it can be difficult to recover data without paying a ransom.

DDoS attacks: Distributed Denial of Service (DDoS) attacks are used to overload a website or network with traffic, causing it to become unavailable to users. DDoS attacks are often carried out using botnets, which are networks of infected devices that are controlled by a hacker.

Man-in-the-middle attacks: A man-in-the-middle (MITM) attack occurs when a cybercriminal intercepts communication between two parties in order to eavesdrop or manipulate the conversation. This can be done through compromised Wi-Fi networks, phishing, or other means.

Password attacks: Password attacks are used to gain unauthorized access to systems or accounts by guessing or stealing passwords. This can be done through brute force attacks, where the attacker tries a large number of passwords, or through phishing attacks, where the attacker tricks the user into revealing their password.

Social engineering: Social engineering is a technique used to manipulate people into revealing sensitive information or performing actions that are not in their best interest. This can be done through phishing, pretexting, baiting, or other methods.

Insider threats: Insider threats occur when someone with authorized access to a system or network intentionally or accidentally causes harm. This can be done through stealing data, introducing malware, or causing system failures.

These are just a few examples of the many cyber threats that exist today. It is important to stay vigilant and take steps to protect yourself and your organization from these and other potential attacks.

Threat actors refer to individuals or groups who engage in activities that pose a potential threat to the security or integrity of an organization or system. Threat actors can be categorized based on their motivation, expertise, and objectives. Some common types of threat actors include:

Hackers: Individuals or groups who use technical expertise to gain unauthorized access to systems, networks, or data.

Cybercriminals: Individuals or groups who engage in illegal activities online, such as stealing personal or financial information, conducting fraud, or distributing malware.

State-sponsored actors: Individuals or groups who are sponsored by a nation-state to conduct espionage or cyberattacks against foreign governments, organizations, or individuals.

Insiders: Employees or contractors who have authorized access to systems or data but misuse their access for personal gain or to cause harm.

Activists: Individuals or groups who use cyberattacks as a means to advance a political or social cause.

It is important for organizations to be aware of different types of threat actors and their tactics, as this can help them develop effective security strategies and mitigate potential risks.

Ethical hacking

Ethical hacking, also known as "white hat ", hacking, is the practice of using hacking techniques to identify and fix security vulnerabilities in computer systems, networks, and applications. Ethical hackers use the same tools and methods as malicious hackers, but they do so with the explicit permission of the system owners and with the goal of improving security rather than causing harm.

The purpose of ethical hacking is to identify weaknesses in security systems before malicious hackers can exploit them. Ethical hackers use various techniques such as vulnerability scanning, penetration testing, and social engineering to uncover vulnerabilities in computer systems and networks. They then report their findings to the system owners so that the vulnerabilities can be fixed before they are exploited by malicious actors.

Ethical hacking is an important practice in today's digital world because of the increasing number of cyber-attacks and the damage they can cause. By identifying and fixing vulnerabilities before they are exploited by malicious actors, ethical hackers can help prevent data breaches, theft of sensitive information, and other types of cyber-attacks.

Ransomware is a type of malicious software (malware) that is designed to encrypt files on a victim's computer, making them inaccessible, and demanding a ransom payment in exchange for the decryption key that would allow the victim to regain access to their files. Ransomware attacks typically begin with the victim being tricked into opening a file or clicking a link in an email or on a website, which then allows the malware to infect their system. Once the malware has encrypted the victim's files, a message will typically appear on their screen demanding payment, often in the form of cryptocurrency, in exchange for the decryption key.

Ransomware attacks have become increasingly common in recent years, and can have serious consequences for individuals, businesses, and organizations of all sizes. Some ransomware strains may even threaten to publicly release sensitive information if the ransom is not paid, adding an additional layer of pressure to the victim. The best way to protect against ransomware is to ensure that your computer and software are up to date with the latest security patches, to use antivirus software, and to exercise caution when opening files or clicking on links from unknown sources.

A botnet is a network of internet-connected devices, such as computers, servers, and IoT devices, which are infected with malware and controlled remotely by a malicious actor. Botnets are typically used for malicious purposes, such as carrying out DDoS attacks, sending spam emails, stealing sensitive data, or distributing malware.

The devices in a botnet are usually infected through malware that exploits vulnerabilities in their software or through social engineering techniques that trick users into downloading and installing malicious software. Once infected, the devices become part of the botnet and can be controlled by the botmaster, who can issue commands to the entire network or to individual devices.

Botnets can be difficult to detect and mitigate, as they are often spread across multiple geographic locations and may use encryption to conceal their communications. However, there are a variety of techniques that can be used to identify and disrupt botnets, such as network traffic analysis, behavioural analysis, and the use of antivirus software and intrusion detection systems.

7.3 – DENIAL OF SERVICE ATTACK

A Denial of Service (DoS) attack is a type of cyber-attack in which an attacker attempts to overwhelm a targeted system or network with traffic, data, or requests to the point where the system becomes unavailable to legitimate users. The attack works by consuming the resources of the targeted system or network, such as CPU usage, bandwidth, or memory, and preventing it from serving legitimate requests.

There are several different types of DoS attacks, including:

Distributed Denial of Service (DDoS) Attack: In this type of attack, the attacker uses a network of compromised devices to flood the targeted system or network with traffic, making it difficult or impossible for legitimate users to access it.

Application Layer Attack: This type of attack targets a specific application or service on the targeted system, overwhelming it with requests or exploiting vulnerabilities in the application to bring it down.

Flood Attack: This type of attack floods the targeted system or network with a large amount of traffic or data, consuming its resources and making it unavailable to legitimate users.

Buffer Overflow Attack: This type of attack exploits a vulnerability in a system or application by sending more data than it can handle, causing it to crash or become unavailable.

To protect against DoS attacks, organizations can implement security measures such as firewalls, intrusion detection and prevention systems, and traffic filtering. It is also important to have an incident response plan in place to quickly identify and mitigate the attack.

7.4 – BOOTKIT AND ROOTKIT MALWARE

A boot kit is a type of malware that infects the boot process of a computer's operating system. It typically targets the Master Boot Record (MBR) or the Unified Extensible Firmware Interface (UEFI) firmware to gain control of the system before the operating system loads.

Boot kits are particularly stealthy and difficult to detect because they operate at a low level, below the operating system and many traditional security tools. Once a boot kit infects a system, it can persist even after the system is rebooted or the hard drive is reformatted.

The goal of a boot kit is usually to give an attacker persistent access to the infected system and to enable them to perform various malicious activities, such as stealing sensitive data, installing additional malware, or controlling the system remotely.

Preventing boot kit infections typically involves using secure boot technologies, keeping firmware, and operating systems up to date, and using security software that can detect and remove boot kits. Additionally, best practices such as not downloading suspicious files or opening attachments from unknown sources can help to prevent boot kit infections.

Rootkit Explained

A rootkit is a type of malicious software or code that is designed to gain privileged access to a computer system or network without being detected. It is usually installed by an attacker who wants to gain unauthorized access to a system or network for malicious purposes, such as stealing sensitive information, spying on users, or controlling the system remotely.

Rootkits are often designed to hide their presence from the operating system and other security software by altering system files, registry entries, or other critical components of the system. This makes them difficult to detect and remove, and they can remain hidden for extended periods of time, allowing the attacker to maintain access and control over the system.

There are different types of rootkits, including kernel-level rootkits, which operate at the level of the operating system kernel, and user-level rootkits, which operate at the user level of the operating system. Some rootkits are also able to hide their presence in memory and can modify their behaviour dynamically to avoid detection.

Rootkits can be installed through a variety of methods, including exploiting vulnerabilities in software or hardware, tricking users into downloading and installing them, or using social engineering techniques to gain access to a system. Protecting your system from rootkits requires a combination of good security practices, such as keeping your software and operating system up to date, using anti-malware software, and being cautious when downloading and installing software from unknown sources.

Email spoofing is a technique used by spammers or scammers to forge the sender's email address in an email message, in order to deceive the recipient into believing that the email is coming from a trusted source. This is done by modifying the email header information, which contains the sender's email address and other details about the message. Spoofed emails can be used for various purposes, such as phishing attacks, spamming, or spreading malware. For example, a phishing email may be disguised as a legitimate email from a bank or other financial institution, and the recipient may be asked to click on a link or provide sensitive information, such as their login credentials or credit card details.

To prevent email spoofing, email service providers and organizations use various techniques, such as SPF (Sender Policy Framework), DKIM (DomainKeys Identified Mail), and DMARC (Domain-based Message Authentication, Reporting, and Conformance). These technologies help to verify the authenticity of the sender's email address and reduce the risk of spoofed emails. Additionally, users can also take precautions, such as avoiding opening suspicious emails, checking the sender's email address, and not clicking on links or downloading attachments from unknown sources.

7.6 – EMAIL BOMBING OR FLOODING

Email bombing, also known as email flooding, is a form of cyber-attack in which a large number of emails are sent to a particular email address or domain, with the intention of overwhelming the recipient's inbox and potentially causing a denial-of-service (DoS) attack.

The emails may contain large attachments, repetitive content, or be sent at a high frequency. This can result in the recipient's email server becoming overloaded and unable to process legitimate email traffic, causing a disruption to their normal operations.

Email bombing is considered a malicious activity and is illegal in many countries. It can cause significant harm to businesses and individuals, including loss of productivity, damage to reputation, and financial losses.

To protect against email bombing, individuals and organizations should implement measures such as using spam filters, limiting the number of messages that can be received from a particular sender, and monitoring email traffic for unusual activity. It is also important to report any instances of email bombing to the relevant authorities.

7.7 – MAN IN THE MIDDLE ATTACK

A man-in-the-middle attack (MITM) is a type of cyber-attack where an attacker intercepts communication between two parties and injects themselves into the conversation without either party knowing. The attacker can then eavesdrop on or modify the communication, potentially stealing sensitive information such as passwords or financial data.

MITM attacks can be carried out through various methods, including:

Spoofing: The attacker creates a fake website or network to intercept the communication.

ARP spoofing: The attacker spoofs the Address Resolution Protocol (ARP) to intercept communication between two devices on a local network.

DNS spoofing: The attacker spoofs the Domain Name System (DNS) to redirect the victim to a fake website.

SSL stripping: The attacker downgrades the secure communication to an unencrypted one, allowing them to intercept and read the communication.

To prevent MITM attacks, it is important to use secure communication protocols, such as HTTPS, and to ensure that software and systems are kept up to date with the latest security patches. It is also important to be cautious when connecting to public Wi-Fi networks, as these are often unsecured and can be used by attackers to carry out MITM attacks.

7.8 – A BACKDOOR THREAT

In computer security, a backdoor is a hidden method of bypassing normal authentication or security controls in a computer system, software application, or network. Backdoors can be intentionally created by software developers or hackers to provide access to a system or network without going through the normal authentication process. Backdoors can also be used to gain access to a system after a password has been changed, or to maintain access to a system after the initial exploit has been discovered and patched.

Backdoors can take many forms, including hidden user accounts, secret commands or key combinations, and hidden network protocols. They can be difficult to detect and can remain hidden for extended periods of time, making them a serious threat to the security of computer systems and networks.

Preventing backdoors requires a multi-layered approach to security, including strong access controls, regular software updates and patching, and ongoing monitoring for suspicious activity. Organizations should also educate their users on best practices for computer security, such as creating strong passwords and avoiding suspicious emails or links.

7.9 – ADVANCED PERSISTENT THREATS

A persistent threat refers to an ongoing and targeted cybersecurity attack that is conducted by an adversary who is highly skilled and well-resourced. These types of threats are characterized by their stealthy and continuous nature, as the attacker often uses sophisticated techniques to evade detection and maintain access to the targeted system or network over an extended period of time.

Persistent threats can take many forms, including malware infections, phishing attacks, and social engineering tactics. The attackers behind persistent threats are often motivated by financial gain, intellectual property theft, or political espionage, and they may target a wide range of organizations, from government agencies and financial institutions to healthcare providers and educational institutions.

To defend against persistent threats, organizations must implement robust cybersecurity measures, such as continuous monitoring, threat hunting, and incident response plans. They must also educate employees on the importance of cybersecurity hygiene and awareness to prevent social engineering attacks, such as phishing. Finally, they must stay up to date with the latest threat intelligence and security technologies to keep pace with the ever-evolving threat landscape.

7.10 ARP ATTACK

An ARP attack, also known as ARP spoofing or ARP poisoning, is a type of cyber-attack where an attacker sends falsified Address Resolution Protocol (ARP) messages over a local area network (LAN).

The goal of an ARP attack is to associate the attacker's MAC address with the IP address of another device on the network, such as the default gateway, so that all traffic intended for that IP address is redirected to the attacker's machine. This can allow the attacker to intercept and read sensitive information, modify network traffic, or even launch further attacks.

ARP attacks can be prevented through the use of various security measures, such as implementing network segmentation, using network intrusion detection systems, and implementing secure ARP protocols. Additionally, using strong encryption and secure communication protocols can help to prevent attackers from intercepting and reading network traffic.

94

A honeypot is a security mechanism used to detect, deflect, or counteract attempts at unauthorized use of information systems.

It involves setting up a system or network with vulnerabilities intentionally, in order to attract and monitor cyber attackers or malicious software, and to gain insights into their methods and motives.

Honeypots can be classified into two types: production honeypots and research honeypots.

Production honeypots are designed to protect production networks and systems by diverting attackers away from critical resources.

Research honeypots, on the other hand, are used for academic and research purposes, and are set up to gather data on attackers' techniques, tactics, and motives.

Honeypots can be used as part of a broader cybersecurity strategy to gather intelligence about potential cyber threats, to improve incident response capabilities, and to provide early warning of attacks. However, honeypots can also pose security risks if they are not properly secured, monitored, and maintained, and can be used as a vector for attackers to gain access to production networks.

Spear phishing is a type of cyber-attack that targets specific individuals or organizations, usually through email or other forms of electronic communication. Unlike regular phishing attacks that are more generic and widespread, spear phishing attacks are highly targeted and personalized. The attackers conduct extensive research on their intended victims to gather information that can be used to make the phishing attempts more convincing and increase the chances of success.

In a spear phishing attack, the attacker typically poses as a trusted individual or entity, such as a colleague, manager, or a well-known organization, to trick the recipient into revealing sensitive information or taking a particular action. The messages or communications used in spear phishing attacks are carefully crafted to appear legitimate and often employ social engineering techniques to manipulate the recipient's emotions or sense of urgency.

Spear phishing attacks can be highly effective because they exploit the trust and familiarity that individuals have with their colleagues or organizations. The attackers may use information gathered from public sources, social media, or previous data breaches to customize their messages and make them more convincing. By tricking victims into providing sensitive information like passwords, credit card numbers, or account credentials, attackers can gain unauthorized access to systems, steal sensitive data, or carry out other malicious activities.

To protect yourself from spear phishing attacks, it is important to be cautious and vigilant while handling emails or other electronic communications. Some recommended practices include:

Verify the sender's identity: Pay attention to the sender's email address and any suspicious or unusual aspects of the message. If you are unsure about the authenticity of an email, contact the supposed sender through a different communication channel to confirm its legitimacy.

Be cautious of unexpected or urgent requests: Spear phishing attacks often create a sense of urgency or exploit emotional triggers to prompt immediate action. Take a moment to verify the request independently before responding or providing any sensitive information.

Think before clicking: Avoid clicking on links or downloading attachments from suspicious or unverified sources. Hover over links to see the actual destination URL before clicking and be wary of shortened URLs or misleading hyperlinks.

Keep software up to date: Regularly update your operating system, antivirus software, web browsers, and other applications to ensure you have the latest security patches and protection against known vulnerabilities.

Be cautious with personal information online: Limit the amount of personal information you share publicly on social media platforms or other online forums. The less information available to attackers, the harder it is for them to personalize their spear phishing attempts.

Educate yourself and stay informed: Stay updated on the latest phishing techniques and security best practices. Organizations often provide awareness training to help their employees recognize and respond to phishing attempts effectively.

By following these practices and maintaining a healthy scepticism towards unsolicited or suspicious communications, you can reduce the risk of falling victim to spear phishing attacks.

S mishing is a form of phishing that is carried out through text messages (SMS) or other messaging platforms like WhatsApp or Viber. It is a type of social engineering attack where the attacker tries to trick individuals into providing sensitive information or performing certain actions by sending fraudulent messages.

The term "smishing" is a combination of "SMS" and "phishing." Like traditional phishing, smishing attempts to deceive victims by posing as a legitimate entity, such as a bank, government agency, or service provider. The messages often contain urgent requests or alarming statements to create a sense of urgency and panic, pushing the recipient to respond quickly without thinking.

Smishing messages typically contain links to fake websites or phone numbers to call, asking for personal information like credit card numbers, social security numbers, passwords, or other sensitive data. The attackers may also attempt to trick victims into downloading malware-infected attachments or apps that can compromise their devices and data.

To protect yourself from smishing attacks, consider the following measures:

Be cautious with messages: Treat unsolicited messages with scepticism, especially those requesting personal information or urgently asking you to act.

Verify the source: Contact the organization directly using a trusted phone number or official website to confirm the authenticity of the message.

Do not click on suspicious links: Avoid clicking on links in messages from unknown or suspicious sources. Hover over the link to see the actual URL before clicking and be cautious even if the link appears legitimate.

Keep your devices updated: Regularly update your smartphone's operating system, applications, and antivirus software to ensure you have the latest security patches.

Install trusted security software: Consider installing reputable mobile security software that can detect and block smishing attempts.

Educate yourself: Stay informed about common phishing and smishing techniques. Learn to recognize red flags and share this knowledge with friends and family to help protect them as well.

Remember, staying vigilant and using common sense when receiving messages can go a long way in preventing falling victim to smishing attacks.

Pharming, also known as phishing with a twist, is a type of cyber-attack that involves the redirection of website traffic to a fraudulent website without the user's knowledge or consent. Unlike traditional phishing, which relies on tricking users into visiting fake websites by clicking on malicious links, pharming manipulates the Domain Name System (DNS) or other network-level vulnerabilities to redirect users to malicious websites.

In a pharming attack, the attacker compromises a DNS server or manipulates the user's local DNS settings, often through malware or DNS cache poisoning. When a user attempts to visit a legitimate website by entering its URL into a web browser, the manipulated DNS settings redirect the request to a fake website that closely resembles the original one. This can lead users to unknowingly enter their sensitive information, such as login credentials, credit card details, or personal information, into the fake website.

The goal of pharming attacks is to deceive users and steal their personal information or engage in other malicious activities. This type of attack can be particularly dangerous because users may not realize they are on a fraudulent website, as the URL and appearance can be convincingly similar to the legitimate website.

To protect against pharming attacks, it is important to keep your computer and devices up to date with security patches, use reliable antivirus software, and exercise caution when clicking on links or downloading files. It is also advisable to regularly check your DNS settings and monitor your online accounts for any suspicious activity.

If you suspect that you have been a victim of a pharming attack or encounter a suspicious website, it is recommended to report it to the appropriate authorities and contact the legitimate website's administrators to alert them of the issue.

Scareware refers to a type of malicious software or deceptive tactics used by cybercriminals to scare or deceive users into taking certain actions that benefit the attacker. The primary goal of scareware is to trick users into believing that their computer is infected with malware or other security threats, and then convincing them to purchase fake or unnecessary software or services.

Scareware typically operates through various methods such as pop-up ads, fake antivirus alerts, and aggressive marketing techniques. Here is a brief overview of how scareware works:

Pop-up Ads: Scareware often utilizes pop-up ads that appear on websites or as system notifications. These ads can be designed to look like legitimate alerts from antivirus software or operating systems, displaying alarming messages such as "Your computer is infected with a virus!" or "Critical system error detected!"

False Security Alerts: Scareware may generate fake security alerts that mimic legitimate antivirus or system notifications. These alerts typically exaggerate or fabricate the presence of malware on the user's computer and urge them to take immediate action.

Deceptive Marketing: Scareware campaigns use aggressive and deceptive marketing tactics to convince users to purchase their products or services. They may claim that their software can remove malware or protect against security threats, but in reality, the software may be ineffective or even harmful.

Rogue Security Software: Scareware often leads users to websites where they are prompted to download or purchase fake antivirus or security software. These programs may have convincing names and interfaces, mimicking legitimate security products. However, they do not provide any real protection and are solely designed to extract money from unsuspecting users.

It is important to note that scareware is malicious and can have harmful consequences. Users who fall victim to scareware may not only waste their money on useless software but also expose their computers to further security risks. To protect yourself from scareware, it is essential to practice safe browsing habits, keep your operating system and antivirus software up to date, and be cautious of unexpected pop-up ads or alerts that appear suspicious.

Vishing, also known as voice phishing, is a type of social engineering attack that uses voice communication, typically over the phone, to deceive individuals into providing sensitive information or performing certain actions. It is a play on the term's "voice" and "phishing," which refers to a similar type of attack conducted through email or other electronic communication.

In a vishing attack, the attacker typically poses as a legitimate entity, such as a bank representative, government agency official, or tech support personnel. They use various tactics to gain the trust of the target and convince them to disclose sensitive information like credit card numbers, social security numbers, login credentials, or other personal and financial details.

Vishing attacks often involve manipulation and social engineering techniques to create a sense of urgency or fear in the target, making them more likely to comply with the attacker's requests. For example, the attacker might claim there has been suspicious activity on the target's account and request immediate action or verification of personal information to resolve the issue.

To protect yourself from vishing attacks, it is essential to be cautious and follow these best practices:

Be sceptical: Be cautious of unsolicited calls, especially if they request sensitive information or ask you to take immediate action.

Verify the caller's identity: If someone claims to be from a particular organization, verify their identity independently. Look up the official contact information and call back using a trusted phone number to ensure you are speaking to a legitimate representative.

Do not provide personal information: Avoid giving out personal or financial information over the phone unless you initiated the call and are confident about the recipient's identity.

Be aware of social engineering tactics: Attackers might try to manipulate you emotionally by creating a sense of urgency, fear, or trust. Stay vigilant and avoid making hasty decisions based solely on such tactics.

Keep software up to date: Regularly update your devices and software to protect against known vulnerabilities that attackers might exploit.

Report suspicious calls: If you receive a suspicious vishing call, report it to the appropriate authorities, such as your local law enforcement or the organization the attacker claimed to represent.

By staying vigilant, being sceptical, and following these precautions, you can reduce the risk of falling victim to vishing attacks.

7.17 – DATA DESTRUCTION

Data destruction attacks refer to malicious activities aimed at destroying or rendering data inaccessible, often with the intention of causing harm or disruption. These attacks can have serious consequences, such as loss of valuable information, financial damage, or disruption of critical services. Here are some common types of data destruction attacks:

Ransomware: Ransomware is a type of malware that encrypts files on a victim's computer or network, rendering them inaccessible. Attackers then demand a ransom payment in exchange for the decryption key. If the victim refuses to pay or cannot recover the files through other means, the data can be permanently lost.

DDoS Attacks: Distributed Denial of Service (DDoS) attacks aim to overwhelm a network, system, or service with a flood of traffic, rendering it inaccessible to legitimate users. While DDoS attacks primarily focus on service disruption, they can indirectly cause data loss or destruction if the targeted systems are not adequately protected.

Data Wiping: In this type of attack, the attacker gains unauthorized access to a system or network and deliberately deletes or wipes out data, rendering it irrecoverable. This can be accomplished through various means, such as exploiting vulnerabilities, using malicious software, or executing targeted commands.

Physical Destruction: Data destruction attacks can also occur through physical means, where an attacker physically damages or destroys the storage devices containing the data. For example, an attacker may physically damage servers, hard drives, or other storage media to render the data inaccessible or unrecoverable.

Insider Threats: Insider threats refer to attacks that originate from within an organization. In some cases, employees or insiders with authorized access may intentionally delete or corrupt data. This can be motivated by various factors, such as revenge, financial gain, or even accidental actions.

Preventing and mitigating data destruction attacks require a multi-layered approach that includes robust security measures, regular backups, access controls, employee awareness training, and incident response plans. It is crucial to have strong cybersecurity practices in place to protect data from such attacks and to implement data recovery mechanisms in case of data loss or destruction.

A buffer overflow attack is a type of security vulnerability that occurs when a program tries to store more data in a buffer (a temporary storage area) than it can handle. This extra data can overflow into adjacent memory locations, corrupting or overwriting the contents of those locations. By carefully crafting the input, an attacker can take advantage of this vulnerability to execute arbitrary code or gain unauthorized access to a system.

Here is a step-by-step explanation of how a buffer overflow attack typically works:

Buffer allocation: The vulnerable program allocates a fixed-size buffer in memory to store data.

Insufficient bounds checking: The program does not perform adequate bounds checking on the data being input. It fails to verify that the input data will fit within the allocated buffer.

Input data overflow: The attacker provides more input data than the buffer can hold, causing the excess data to overflow into adjacent memory locations.

Overwriting memory: The overflowed data can overwrite important data structures, such as function pointers, return addresses, or control variables, with malicious values.

Exploiting control flow: By manipulating the overwritten values, the attacker can redirect the execution flow of the program to execute their own code.

Execution of malicious code: The attacker's code, typically called the payload, is executed with the privileges of the vulnerable program. This can lead to various consequences, such as remote code execution, denial of service, privilege escalation, or unauthorized access.

Buffer overflow attacks can be highly dangerous and are a common target for attackers. To mitigate the risk of such attacks, software developers should implement secure coding practices, including proper input validation, bounds checking, and using secure programming libraries and techniques. Additionally, operating system vendors and security researchers work to identify and patch vulnerabilities to prevent buffer overflow attacks. Regularly updating software and systems can help protect against known vulnerabilities.

7.19 – DATA INTERCEPTING AND SESSION HIJACKING

Interception of data refers to the act of capturing or acquiring digital information during its transmission or storage. This interception can occur through various means, including electronic surveillance, hacking, or unauthorized access to networks or devices. The purpose of data interception can range from monitoring communications for legitimate purposes like law enforcement or intelligence gathering to malicious activities such as identity theft or industrial espionage.

There are different methods and techniques used to intercept data, depending on the context and the level of sophistication involved. Here are a few common methods:

Network Sniffing: Attackers can use tools or software to monitor network traffic and capture data packets as they pass through the network. This can be done by gaining access to a compromised device or by setting up malicious software on the network.

Man-in-the-Middle (MitM) Attacks: In a MitM attack, an attacker positions themselves between two communicating parties, intercepting, and altering the data being exchanged. This can be achieved by compromising network routers, DNS servers, or by leveraging vulnerabilities in protocols or encryption.

Phishing: Phishing attacks involve tricking individuals into providing their sensitive information, such as usernames, passwords, or financial details, through fraudulent websites or emails. Attackers can intercept this data by mimicking legitimate platforms and capturing the information entered by unsuspecting users.

Malware: Malicious software, such as keyloggers or spyware, can be used to intercept and capture data on infected devices. These programs can record keystrokes, take screenshots, or capture other sensitive information without the user's knowledge.

Data Breaches: Data breaches occur when an unauthorized party gains access to a system or database and steals sensitive information. This can happen due to vulnerabilities in the system, weak passwords, or insider threats.

To protect against data interception, it is important to implement robust security measures, including:

Encryption: Encrypting data before transmission ensures that even if intercepted, the information remains unreadable and unusable without the decryption key.

Secure Protocols: Using secure communication protocols, such as HTTPS for web traffic, helps protect data in transit from interception.

Firewalls and Intrusion Detection Systems: These systems can monitor network traffic and detect and block unauthorized access attempts.

Strong Authentication: Implementing multi-factor authentication and using strong passwords helps prevent unauthorized access to sensitive data.

Regular Updates and Patches: Keeping software and systems up to date with the latest security patches helps mitigate vulnerabilities that could be exploited for data interception.

It is important for individuals and organizations to stay informed about emerging threats and maintain proactive security practices to minimize the risk of data interception and protect sensitive information.

Session hijacking, also known as session stealing or session side jacking, refers to the unauthorized takeover of a user's active session on a computer system or web application. In session hijacking, an attacker intercepts and gains control over the session identifier or token that is used to authenticate and maintain a user's session. By doing so, the attacker can impersonate the legitimate user and perform actions on their behalf without their knowledge or consent.

There are various methods that attackers can employ to hijack sessions:

Packet Sniffing: Attackers use packet sniffing techniques to capture network traffic and extract session information, such as session cookies or tokens, from unencrypted connections. Once they have obtained the session identifier, they can use it to impersonate the user.

Session Side jacking: This method involves eavesdropping on a user's network communication, typically on public Wi-Fi networks. Attackers can use tools like Wireshark to intercept and capture session cookies or tokens sent over the network.

Cross-Site Scripting (XSS): If a website is vulnerable to XSS attacks, an attacker can inject malicious scripts into the website, which are then executed by the victims' browsers. These scripts can be used to steal session information, including session cookies, and transmit them to the attacker.

Session Fixation: In session fixation attacks, an attacker tricks a user into using a predetermined session identifier. For example, they might send a malicious link to the victim, which contains a session identifier that the attacker already knows. When the user clicks on the link and logs in, the attacker can then use the fixed session identifier to hijack the session.

Once an attacker successfully hijacks a session, they can perform various malicious activities, such as accessing sensitive information, manipulating user data, conducting fraudulent transactions, or even escalating their privileges within the system.

To protect against session hijacking, it is essential to implement secure practices such as:

Use secure and encrypted communication protocols like HTTPS to prevent packet sniffing attacks.

Implement secure session management techniques, including random and unpredictable session identifiers, session timeouts, and session token rotation.

Employ secure coding practices to prevent cross-site scripting (XSS) vulnerabilities.

Regularly update and patch web applications to fix security vulnerabilities.

Use strong and secure session cookies, such as HTTP-only and secure flags, to protect against session theft.

Educate users about the risks of using public Wi-Fi networks and encourage the use of VPNs (Virtual Private Networks) to encrypt their internet traffic.

By adopting these measures, both web application developers and users can reduce the risk of session hijacking and enhance the security of their online sessions.

7.20 – MALFORMED URL ATTACKS

A malformed URL attack, also known as a URL injection attack or a URL-based attack, is a type of security vulnerability where an attacker manipulates a URL to exploit a vulnerability in a web application or system. By crafting a malicious URL, the attacker aims to deceive the application or system into performing unintended actions or revealing sensitive information.

Here are a few examples of common malformed URL attacks:

Path Traversal: The attacker manipulates the URL to traverse directories and access files or directories outside of the intended scope. For example, they may append "../" sequences to the URL to move up the directory hierarchy.

Directory Listing: If a web server is not properly configured, an attacker can force the server to display a directory listing instead of the intended webpage by manipulating the URL. This can expose sensitive files and directories to unauthorized access.

SQL Injection: By injecting SQL statements into the URL parameters, an attacker can manipulate the underlying database of a web application. This can allow them to extract or modify data, or even execute arbitrary commands on the database server.

Cross-Site Scripting (XSS): Attackers can inject malicious scripts into URLs that are displayed on a website. When a user clicks on the manipulated URL, the script is executed in their browser, allowing the attacker to steal sensitive information or perform actions on the user's behalf.

Command Injection: In some cases, a web application might allow certain commands to be executed on the server through the URL. An attacker can exploit this by injecting additional commands into the URL, potentially gaining unauthorized access to the server, or performing malicious actions.

Preventing Malformed URL attacks typically involves implementing proper input validation and sanitization techniques within the web application. Here are a few preventive measures:

Input Validation: Validate and sanitize all user-supplied input, including URL parameters, before using them in any application logic or database queries. This helps to prevent unintended interpretation of malicious input.

Whitelisting: Implement a strict whitelist of allowable characters and patterns for URL parameters. This helps to filter out any potentially malicious input.

URL Encoding: Properly encode and decode URL parameters to ensure that special characters are handled correctly and do not lead to unintended behaviour.

Server Configuration: Configure web servers to disable directory listing and restrict access to sensitive files and directories. Ensure that default settings are properly modified to enhance security.

Security Testing: Regularly conduct security assessments, including vulnerability scanning and penetration testing, to identify and address any vulnerabilities in the web application.

It is important to stay vigilant and keep your web applications and systems updated with the latest security patches to mitigate the risk of malformed URL attacks and other security vulnerabilities.

7.21 – QUISHING OR QR CODE ATTACKS

QR code phishing or Quishing is a type of cyberattack where malicious QR codes are used to deceive individuals into visiting fraudulent websites or downloading malicious apps. Attackers often disguise these QR codes in a way that appears legitimate, such as on flyers, posters, or even emails. When scanned, the QR code leads the user to a phishing website designed to steal sensitive information like login credentials or personal data.

To protect yourself from QR code phishing:

Use a Trusted QR Code Scanner: Download a reputable QR code scanner app from a trusted source to minimize the risk of scanning malicious codes.

Examine the QR Code: Before scanning, visually inspect the QR code for any suspicious elements or unusual URLs. If it seems suspicious, avoid scanning it.

Stay Cautious: Be cautious when scanning QR codes from unknown sources, especially if you did not expect to receive one.

Verify the URL: After scanning, review the URL before entering any personal information. Ensure it matches the legitimate website's domain.

Keep Software Updated: Keep your smartphone's operating system and apps up to date to patch security vulnerabilities.

Use Multi-Factor Authentication (MFA): Enable MFA whenever possible to add an extra layer of security to your online accounts.

Educate Yourself: Stay informed about the latest phishing techniques and cybersecurity best practices to protect yourself and others.

By following these precautions, you can reduce the risk of falling victim to QR code phishing attacks.

Here are some key points about hot-mike attacks:

A hot mike refers to a microphone that is accidentally left on and transmitting audio without the speaker's knowledge. This makes it vulnerable to attack.

Hot-mike attacks involve hackers exploiting unintentionally activated microphones in devices to eavesdrop and collect sensitive audio data.

Common targets include smartphones, laptops, smart speakers, and other IoT devices with microphones. Even virtual assistants like Siri, Alexa and Google Assistant could be vulnerable.

The microphone can be activated remotely by malware or a malicious app that bypasses security settings. Physical access to the device may not be required.

Captured private conversations, phone calls, meetings, and other audio can then be sent to the hacker. This compromises privacy and allows data theft.

These attacks demonstrate the need for better indicator lights and permissions around microphone access. Disabling microphone access when not actively using voice features can also help prevent hot-mike attacks.

Companies and users should be aware of this threat and take steps to guard against it through device security, settings management, and microphone discipline. Audio data can be highly sensitive.

In summary, hot-mike attacks exploit always-on microphone access in today's devices and represent a concerning risk to privacy and security. Preventative measures are required.

7.23 – SUPPLY-CHAIN ATTACKS

Here are some key things to know about supply chain attacks in cybersecurity:

A supply chain attack targets an organization or software/hardware product through its supply chain dependencies and third-party elements.

Attackers may compromise a supplier, vendor or partner network and plant malware, a backdoor or other vulnerability that gives them access.

The goal is to infiltrate the ultimate target's systems and data by moving laterally through its trusted supply chain.

Examples include compromising software updates, injecting malware into software dependencies, hardware-level implants, and poisoning code repositories.

Major supply chain attacks have targeted SolarWinds, Kaseya, Codecov and open-source repositories like npm and PyPI.

These attacks are increasing as more businesses rely on complex I.T. supply chains and software distributions.

Preventative measures involve supply chain risk management, monitoring third-party access, vetting suppliers, diversifying vendors, auditing code, and updating regularly.

Companies should aim for end-to-end supply chain visibility, control, and diversity. Staying on top of updates and patches is also key.

In summary, supply chain attacks represent an insidious threat today through third-party compromise. Strong supplier security and supply chain hygiene are crucial to mitigate this risk.

7.24 – AI-POWERED CYBER ATTACKS

Here are some key points about AI-powered cybersecurity attacks: AI can be misused by attackers to automate, optimize and scale cyberattacks more effectively.

AI techniques like machine learning allow attackers to analyse volumes of data, adapt to defences, evade detection, and exploit vulnerabilities in software or networks.

Examples include using AI for smarter spear phishing, credential stuffing, generating disinformation, finding bugs in code, and automating different attack vectors.

Attackers may also use AI to analyse large sets of stolen data and information to gain insights faster. This makes data breaches more lucrative.

On the defence side, AI is being used for pattern recognition to detect emerging attacks, automated threat intelligence, and analysing security data at scale.

Overall, there is an "AI arms race" emerging in cybersecurity between attackers and defenders.

As AI advances, attacks and defences will become more sophisticated and automated. This may expand the threat landscape.

To mitigate risks, security teams need AI expertise, continuous training of AI systems, multi-layered defences, and collaboration between humans and AI.

In summary, while AI brings many benefits, it also empowers adversaries. Proactive efforts are required to guard against AI-enhanced cyberattacks and ensure security keeps pace.

A keylogger is a type of surveillance technology used to monitor and record each keystroke typed on a specific computer. Here are some key details about keyloggers:

They record all keyboard input, including passwords, emails, messages, and any other text typed by a user.

Keyloggers save this data locally or transmit it covertly to a remote receiver.

They are used both by cybercriminals for stealing sensitive data as well as lawfully to monitor employees or minor children.

Keyloggers can be software installed on a computer, a physical device plugged in between the computer and keyboard, or a script run remotely.

Signs of a possible keylogger include keyboard malfunctions, unusual activity lights, strange connections, and performance issues.

Anti-virus software can detect and remove some keyloggers. But advanced ones using rootkits can evade detection.

Best practices to prevent keyloggers include covering webcams, keeping software updated, avoiding unauthorized downloads, and scanning regularly with anti-virus software.

Users should also watch for suspicious behaviour like encrypted traffic, unfamiliar processes or programs running, and unexplained disk space usage.

Keylogger evidence is legally admissible only if installed by authorized parties like parents or employers monitoring their own systems.

Overall, keyloggers represent a powerful surveillance threat that users should be knowledgeable about in order to detect and mitigate.

8. CYBER SECURITY STRATEGIES

The Cyber Kill Chain is a model that outlines the different stages of a cyberattack, from the initial reconnaissance to the final stage of exfiltration or destruction of data. The model was originally developed by Lockheed Martin as a framework to help organizations understand and defend against advanced persistent threats (APTs).

The Cyber Kill Chain model consists of the following seven stages:

Reconnaissance: This is the initial stage where the attacker gathers information about the target. This may involve scanning the target's network, researching the target's employees or partners, or even visiting the target's physical location to gather information.

Weaponization: In this stage, the attacker creates or acquires a weapon (such as malware) that can be used to exploit a vulnerability in the target's network or system.

Delivery: The weapon is delivered to the target, often through a phishing email or a drive-by download.

Exploitation: The weapon is activated to exploit the vulnerability, allowing the attacker to gain access to the target's system.

Installation: Once access has been gained, the attacker installs additional tools or malware to maintain persistence and expand their access to the target's system.

Command and Control (C2): The attacker establishes a command-and-control infrastructure to communicate with the compromised system and issue commands.

Actions on Objectives: Finally, the attacker acts on their objectives, which may include stealing sensitive data, disrupting operations, or causing damage to the target's system.

By understanding the different stages of the Cyber Kill Chain, organizations can implement proactive measures to detect and prevent attacks before they reach the final stage. This can include measures such as network segmentation, intrusion detection and prevention systems, and employee training on security awareness and best practices.

Penetration testing, also known as pen testing or ethical hacking, is the practice of testing a computer system, network or web application to find security vulnerabilities that an attacker could exploit. Here are some key points about pen testing:

The goal is to identify security weaknesses before malicious hackers can find and abuse them. Pen testing aims to improve security proactively.

Tests are performed by authorized cybersecurity professionals called penetration testers or white hat hackers. They use hacking techniques and tools to simulate real-world attacks.

Activities typically include network scanning, vulnerability assessment, exploiting identified flaws to gain access, and social engineering. Tests can focus on network, web app, cloud, etc.

Penetration testers follow a defined scope and rules of engagement. The goal is to compromise security without causing damage or disruption.

After the test, pen testers provide a detailed report on vulnerabilities found and how to remediate them. They also share recommendations to improve overall security.

Penetration tests should be performed regularly, such as annually or whenever major infrastructure changes occur. Ongoing testing identifies new vulnerabilities that arise over time.

Companies commonly outsource pen testing to specialized cybersecurity firms. Tests can also be conducted internally by experienced security engineers.

Benefits include identifying unknown security gaps, meeting compliance requirements, improving incident response, and keeping cyber defences updated. But it requires technical expertise.

9 – TOR AND THE DARK WEB

TOR stands for "The Onion Router" and it is a free and open-source software designed to provide online anonymity by routing internet traffic through a network of servers operated by volunteers around the world.

When using TOR, your internet traffic is encrypted and sent through a series of TOR nodes, also known as relays, before it reaches its destination. Each node in the chain only knows the identity of the previous and next nodes, which makes it difficult to trace the origin of the traffic.

TOR is commonly used by individuals who want to protect their privacy and avoid online surveillance. It is also used by activists, journalists, and whistle-blowers who need to communicate securely and anonymously. However, TOR can also be used for illegal activities such as accessing the dark web and buying or selling drugs, weapons, or stolen information.

The dark web refers to the portion of the internet that is not indexed by traditional search engines and is only accessible through specific software or configurations. It is often used for illicit activities, such as illegal marketplaces, cybercrime, and online forums for extremist groups.

The dark web is made up of hidden services that use the Tor network, which is a network of servers and clients designed to provide anonymity and privacy to users. Tor is often used by individuals who wish to remain anonymous, such as journalists, activists, and whistle-blowers, but it can also be used for nefarious purposes.

While the dark web has gained notoriety for illegal activities, it is important to note that not everything on the dark web is illegal or harmful. There are also legitimate uses for the dark web, such as providing a platform for free speech in countries with strict censorship laws or allowing individuals to communicate anonymously for safety reasons.

It is important to exercise caution when accessing the dark web, as it is not regulated and can pose significant risks to personal privacy and security. Users should only access the dark web with a strong understanding of the potential risks and with appropriate security measures in place.

10 – CRYPTOCURRENCY

10.1 - Cryptocurrency Overview

Cryptocurrency refers to a digital or virtual form of currency that utilizes cryptography for security. It is designed to work as a medium of exchange, just like traditional currencies such as the US dollar or the Euro, but it exists solely in electronic form.

Unlike centralized currencies issued and regulated by governments (known as fiat currencies), cryptocurrencies are typically decentralized and operate on a technology called blockchain. A blockchain is a distributed ledger that records all transactions across a network of computers, ensuring transparency, security, and immutability.

Cryptocurrencies employ cryptographic techniques to secure transactions and control the creation of new units. They use advanced mathematics and encryption to regulate the generation of new units and verify the transfer of assets. This decentralized nature, along with cryptographic security, makes cryptocurrencies resistant to fraud and manipulation.

The most well-known cryptocurrency is Bitcoin, which was introduced in 2009 by the mysterious Satoshi Nakamoto. However, numerous other cryptocurrencies, often referred to as altcoins, have emerged since then, each with its own unique features and purposes. Some popular altcoins include Ethereum, Ripple, Litecoin, and many others.

Cryptocurrencies offer various potential benefits, such as faster and cheaper cross-border transactions, increased privacy, elimination of intermediaries, and the potential for decentralized applications and smart contracts. However, they also carry risks, including price volatility, regulatory uncertainties, and the potential for use in illegal activities.

It is important to note that the cryptocurrency landscape is constantly evolving, and new developments, technologies, and regulations can significantly impact the understanding and usage of cryptocurrencies.

Ethereum is a decentralised blockchain platform that enables the creation and execution of smart contracts. As with any digital system, security is a critical aspect of Ethereum to ensure the integrity, confidentiality, and availability of the network and its associated assets. Here are some key aspects of Ethereum security:

Cryptographic Security: Ethereum relies on cryptographic algorithms to secure its transactions and data. Public-key cryptography is used to ensure the authenticity and integrity of transactions, while encryption techniques protect sensitive information stored on the network.

Consensus Mechanism: Ethereum currently uses a consensus mechanism called Proof of Stake (PoS) called Ethereum 2.0 (or Eth2). It replaces the previous Proof of Work (PoW) mechanism used in Ethereum 1.0. PoS relies on validators who hold and "stake" their Ethereum to secure the network and validate transactions. This mechanism improves security by making it economically expensive for attackers to compromise the network.

Smart Contract Security: Smart contracts on the Ethereum platform are self-executing programs that automatically execute the terms of an agreement. However, they can be vulnerable to bugs, coding errors, or security flaws. The Ethereum community actively promotes secure coding practices and conducts regular audits of smart contracts to identify vulnerabilities and reduce the risk of exploits.

Security Audits: Independent security audits are conducted by specialized firms to review the code and architecture of critical Ethereum components, such as smart contracts, wallets, and decentralized applications (DApps). These audits aim to identify potential vulnerabilities, assess risks, and provide recommendations to improve security.

Bug Bounty Programs: Ethereum and various projects within the Ethereum ecosystem often establish bug bounty programs. These programs incentivise security researchers and developers to discover and report vulnerabilities in the system. By offering rewards for finding and responsibly disclosing bugs, these programs help to identify and fix security issues before they can be exploited by malicious actors.

Community Vigilance: The Ethereum community plays a vital role in maintaining the network's security. Participants are encouraged to report suspicious activities, share information about potential threats, and collaborate on security-related initiatives. Public discussion forums and specialized channels allow the community to stay vigilant and address security concerns promptly.

Network Upgrades: Ethereum regularly undergoes upgrades and protocol improvements to enhance its security and performance. These upgrades may introduce changes to the consensus mechanism, implement new cryptographic standards, or address known vulnerabilities. The community's active involvement and support are crucial in adopting these upgrades and maintaining a secure network.

While Ethereum employs various security measures, it is essential to note that no system is entirely immune to security risks. As the technology evolves, new vulnerabilities may arise, requiring ongoing efforts to address emerging threats and ensure the long-term security of the Ethereum ecosystem.

10.3 - Cryptocurrency Security Best Practices

Cryptocurrency security is a crucial aspect of the digital asset ecosystem. As cryptocurrencies are decentralized and digital in nature, their security relies on a combination of cryptographic techniques, secure protocols, and responsible user practices. Here are some key aspects of cryptocurrency security:

Wallet Security: Cryptocurrency wallets are used to store and manage digital assets. There are different types of wallets, including hardware wallets, software wallets, and online wallets. It is important to choose a reputable wallet provider and ensure that your wallet is properly secured with strong passwords and two-factor authentication (2FA) where available. Hardware wallets, such as Ledger or Trezor, provide an added layer of security by keeping private keys offline.

Private Key Management: Private keys are essential for accessing and transferring cryptocurrencies. It is crucial to keep your private keys secure and not share them with anyone. Ideally, store your private keys in offline and encrypted environments, such as hardware wallets or paper wallets. Avoid storing them in digital form on devices connected to the internet, as they can be vulnerable to hacking.

Two-Factor Authentication (2FA): Enabling 2FA adds an extra layer of security to your cryptocurrency accounts. This feature typically requires you to provide a secondary verification method, such as a code from an authentication app or a physical security key, in addition to your password when logging in or making transactions.

Secure Networks and Devices: Use secure and trusted networks when accessing your cryptocurrency accounts. Avoid using public Wi-Fi networks, which can be susceptible to eavesdropping and attacks. Ensure your devices, including computers and smartphones, have up-to-date antivirus software and operating system patches to mitigate potential vulnerabilities.

Phishing Awareness: Be cautious of phishing attempts where malicious actors try to trick you into revealing your sensitive information, such as passwords or private keys, through fake websites or emails. Always verify the authenticity of the websites you visit and be wary of unsolicited communications asking for your confidential information.

Regular Updates and Security Practices: Stay updated with the latest security practices and news related to cryptocurrencies. Follow security recommendations provided by cryptocurrency projects, wallet providers, and exchanges. Regularly update your software wallets and applications to benefit from the latest security patches.

Research and Due Diligence: Before investing in a cryptocurrency, conduct a thorough research about the project, its team, and the security measures they have in place. Choose reputable exchanges and platforms for trading and ensure they have proper security protocols, such as cold storage for funds and strong user authentication.

Backup and Recovery: Regularly back up your wallets and store the backup securely. This ensures that you can recover your cryptocurrencies in case of device loss, damage, or theft. Keep in mind that losing access to your private keys without a backup can result in a permanent loss of funds.

Remember, cryptocurrency security is a shared responsibility. While these measures can enhance the security of your digital assets, it is important to stay vigilant and practice good security habits to protect yourself from potential threats.

Hardware wallets are physical devices designed to securely store and manage cryptocurrency private keys offline. They provide an extra layer of security compared to software wallets or exchanges, as they keep the private keys isolated from internet-connected devices, which reduces the risk of online attacks and malware.

Here are some key aspects of hardware wallet security:

Private Key Isolation: Hardware wallets store private keys offline within the device itself and never expose them to the computer or the internet. This isolation ensures that the keys are protected even if the computer used for transactions is compromised.

Secure Element: Hardware wallets often incorporate a secure element, such as a specialized chip, which provides additional protection against tampering and extraction of private keys. The secure element helps safeguard the keys from physical attacks.

PIN Protection: Hardware wallets typically require a PIN code to access the device. This PIN acts as an extra layer of security and prevents unauthorized access in case the device is lost or stolen.

Backup and Recovery: Hardware wallets generate a recovery seed or mnemonic phrase—a sequence of words that represents the private keys. This seed serves as a backup and allows users to restore their wallet on another compatible device if the original one is lost or damaged.

Verification of Transactions: When making a transaction, hardware wallets often display the details of the transaction on the device's screen. Users can verify the transaction details on the device before confirming it, ensuring that they are sending funds to the intended recipient and the correct amount.

Open Source and Audits: Some hardware wallets are open source, allowing the community to review the code for security vulnerabilities. Additionally, reputable hardware wallet manufacturers may undergo third-party audits or security assessments to validate the robustness of their devices.

Firmware Updates: Manufacturers regularly release firmware updates for hardware wallets. These updates often include security patches, bug fixes, and additional features. Keeping the firmware up to date is crucial to benefit from the latest security improvements.

Physical Security: Hardware wallets are designed to be physically durable and resistant to tampering. However, users should still handle and store them in secure locations, protecting them from theft, damage, or unauthorized access.

While hardware wallets significantly enhance security, it is essential to be cautious while purchasing them. Always buy hardware wallets directly from reputable sources to minimize the risk of receiving tampered or counterfeit devices.

Remember, no security measure is entirely fool proof, and it is important to exercise caution when using any type of cryptocurrency wallet. Following best practices, such as regularly updating firmware, backing up your recovery seed in a secure manner, and being aware of phishing attempts, will help maximize the security of your cryptocurrency holdings.

10.4.1 – Why use a hardware wallet?

Here are some of the key reasons to use a hardware wallet to store cryptocurrency:

Enhanced security - Private keys are stored offline on the device rather than on a computer or mobile device that is vulnerable to hacking. This makes it much harder for keys to be compromised.

Control - Hardware wallets empower users to have full control of their funds. Users have the peace of mind that no one can transfer funds without physical access to the hardware wallet.

Backup and recovery - Many hardware wallets provide backup and restore mechanisms to enable recovery of funds in case the device is lost, stolen or damaged.

Support many cryptocurrencies - A single hardware wallet can store a variety of cryptocurrencies instead of needing a unique wallet for each. Devices support major coins like Bitcoin, Ethereum, and others.

Ease of use - Hardware wallets provide an easy-to-use way to securely store crypto and make transactions without dealing with complex cryptography. The device manages the technical aspects.

Accessibility - Wallets allow users to easily access and transact with their cryptocurrency holdings from any computer or smartphone. Keys stay protected on device.

Cold storage - Keys are generated and stay offline on the device instead of being stored on internet-connected devices vulnerable to hacking.

Portability - Hardware wallets are small and portable enough to carry conveniently with you. The private keys go where you go.

Compatibility - Most hardware wallets easily integrate with various wallets and software a user may want to use.

The bottom line is that hardware wallets currently provide the most secure and convenient way for average users to protect their cryptocurrency. The benefits in security, backup, and usability make them a worthwhile investment.

About the Author

Brian is a cybersecurity professional, graduated with a Masters degree in Cybersecurity and Digital Forensics from Edinburgh Napier University in 2019. He is a Cybersecurity consultant with the Scotcoin Project since his University days in 2016. Brian has worked in IT industry since 1997 when he worked as a first line support at BT Internet helpdesk.